Beethoven: The 'Moonlight' and other Sonatas, Op. 27 and Op. 31

Timothy Jones

Lecturer in Music, University of Exeter

CAMBRIDGE
UNIVERSITY PRESS

PUBLISHED BY THE PRESS SYNDICATE OF THE UNIVERSITY OF CAMBRIDGE
The Pitt Building, Trumpington Street, Cambridge CB2 1RP, United Kingdom

CAMBRIDGE UNIVERSITY PRESS
The Edinburgh Building, Cambridge CB2 2RU, UK   http://www.cup.cam.ac.uk
40 West 20th Street, New York, NY 10011-4211, USA   http://www.cup.org
10 Stamford Road, Oakleigh, Melbourne 3166, Australia

First published 1999

Printed in the United Kingdom at the University Press, Cambridge

Typeset in Ehrhardt MT 10½/13pt, in QuarkXPress™   [SE]

A catalogue record for this book is available from the British Library

Library of Congress cataloguing in publication data

Jones, Timothy, Dr.
Beethoven, the 'Moonlight' and other sonatas, op. 27 and op. 31 /
Timothy Jones.
p.   cm. – (Cambridge music handbooks)
Includes bibliographical references and index.
ISBN 0 521 59136 8 (hardback). – ISBN 0 521 59859 1 (paperback)
1. Beethoven, Ludwig van, 1770–1827. Sonatas, piano, no. 14–18.
2. Sonatas (Piano) – Analysis, appreciation. I. Series.
ML410.B42J66   1999
786.2'183–dc21   98-45826   CIP   MN

ISBN 0 521 59136 8 hardback
ISBN 0 521 59859 1 paperback

CAMBRIDGE MUSIC HANDBOOKS

Beethoven: The 'Moonlight' and other Sonatas Op. 27 and Op. 31

CAMBRIDGE MUSIC HANDBOOKS

GENERAL EDITOR   Julian Rushton

Recent titles

To Mummy Hetty

Contents

Preface

'Everyone always talks about the C♯ minor Sonata!' exclaimed Beethoven in a moment of exasperation. And, confronted with the vast literature on this sonata, it seems that everyone has continued to talk and write about the 'Moonlight' from the composer's day to our own. Why add to that body of work? First, most of the material on the sonata is inaccessible to all but the most dedicated researcher, and there is currently no monograph on the work in English. Second, there has been much recent scholarly work on Beethoven's first decade in Vienna (1792–1802), and advances in our understanding of the composer's early career are bound to change the way we perceive the works he wrote around the turn of the century. In response, this study engages in a reassessment of the 'Moonlight' Sonata's place in Beethoven's work.

To do so it has been necessary to emulate the sonata and break with a tradition. Unlike the other Cambridge Music Handbooks this book focuses neither on a single work nor on a complete repertoire. My decision to discuss two sets of sonatas dating from 1801–3 has been motivated by historiographical as well as critical factors. The efficacy of perceiving Beethoven's life in early, middle and late periods has been challenged by Beethoven scholars in the last few decades, but it is still universally recognised that the years 1801–3 were crucial for his development as a composer. At the start of the nineteenth century, Beethoven had established himself as the leading piano virtuoso-composer in Vienna after a decade in the city, but had suffered a setback with the dawning realisation that the decline in his hearing was irreversible. At the same time, his music – which had always been perceived by his contemporaries as individual and difficult – became more original, cutting loose from classical models and pointing the way to later masterpieces such as the 'Eroica' and Fifth Symphonies, the 'Waldstein' and

'Appassionata' Sonatas, and the Op. 59 String Quartets. By the end of 1802 fifteen of Beethoven's piano sonatas had been published, and five more had been composed:

	Written	Published
2	1793–5	1796
Op. 49	1795–7	1805
Op. 7	1796–7	1797
Op. 10	1796–8	1798
Op. 13	1797–8	1799
Op. 14	1798–9	1799
Op. 22	1800	1802
Op. 26	1800–1	1802
Op. 27	1801–2	1802
Op. 28	1802	1802
Op. 31	1802	1803–4

With the exception of Op. 49, these sonatas display a marked individuality that pushes at the generic and stylistic boundaries of the classical genre. But in two sets of sonatas from 1801–2 Beethoven was more radically innovative. In the two Op. 27 pieces he created a new subgenre, the fantasy sonata, by amalgamating late-eighteenth-century sonata and fantasy styles; and in the three Op. 31 sonatas he began to rethink fundamental aspects of classical musical syntax itself. The aim of this study is therefore to explore two contrasting ways in which Beethoven distanced himself from his classical heritage at this crucial stage in his career.

It is difficult to understand what Beethoven was trying to achieve in these works without first considering his Viennese milieu and trends in keyboard music during the 1790s. Chapter 1 gives a brief outline of the keyboard culture of Beethoven's day and discusses the aesthetic values held by the composer's aristocratic sponsors, and chapter 2 considers the changes of direction in Beethoven's career and music at the start of the century. Chapter 3 gives an overview of the genesis and after-life of the sonatas. The final three chapters address technical and critical issues in more detail: chapter 4 explores what the title 'Sonata *quasi una fantasia*' might have meant to Beethoven's contemporaries; chapters 5 and 6 give brief analytical accounts of the sonatas. Of course it is impossible in a Handbook to begin to do justice to works of such richness and complexity. My analyses are designed to suggest avenues for more detailed inquiry rather than as fully rounded readings of the sonatas. If their omissions infuriate you, then hopefully the provocation will be fruitful.

Due to limitations of space, music examples have been kept to a minimum. Readers will find it helpful to follow chapters 5 and 6 with a score. Many editions of the sonatas are heavily encrusted with editorial additions and alterations: references in chapters 5 and 6 are to the Henlé Edition of the sonatas, edited by Hans Schmidt. Throughout the text, specific pitches are identified according to the Helmholtz system, C–B, c–b, c^1–b^1, c^2–b^2, etc., whereby c^1 = 'middle' C. Where pitches are discussed in terms of their functions as scale degrees (their position within the scale of the prevailing key), they are signified by a number with a superscript caret: for example, G is $\hat{1}$ in G, but $\hat{3}$ in E♭. In the discussion of harmonic functions, upper-case letters denote major keys and lower-case letters minor keys. The abbreviation V/d means the dominant of D minor.

Acknowledgements

I am indebted to Julian Rushton and Penny Souster for their encouragement and patience while this book gestated. Thanks are due to the staffs at the University Library, Exeter; the Music Faculty Library and Bodleian Library, Oxford; the British Library, London; the Bibliothèque Nationale, Paris; and the Staatsbibliothek Preussischer Kulturbesitz, Berlin. I am grateful to my Exeter colleagues Richard Langham Smith, Alan Street and Ian Mitchell for their comments and advice; also to the students at St Peter's College, Oxford and Exeter University who have been subjected to my developing thoughts on these sonatas in the last few years. Among many friends who have generously read, listened, and advised, special thanks go to Susanna Stranders, Richard Cross, Essaka Joshua, Susan Wollenberg, Elizabeth Norman McKay, Gilbert McKay and Emma Dillon. The support of my family has been a constant strength. My Grandmother gave me her copy of a rare nineteenth-century edition of Beethoven's sonatas when I was much too young to appreciate its value. In return, this book is dedicated to her.

1

Keyboard culture

Pianos came of age in Beethoven's formative years. During the last quarter of the eighteenth century, they rivalled and eventually superseded harpsichords and clavichords as the favoured domestic and concert keyboard instrument. As the wealth of mercantile families in England and central Europe grew, so did the market for the new instruments. To meet the demands of this unprecedented mass cultural phenomenon, a vast body of music exploiting the instrument's unique properties was written (largely for domestic consumption), and the publication of sheet music proliferated. The crest of this wave was ridden by virtuoso pianist-composers who built their careers on three core skills: their technical brilliance as performers, their outstanding abilities at extempore improvisation, and their fluency as composers. Mozart and Clementi (born in 1752) blazed the trail in the early 1780s, and in the next twenty years a number of virtuosi came to prominence. In addition to Beethoven, the outstanding figures at the turn of the century were (in order of birth) Jan Ladislav Dussek (1760), Daniel Steibelt (1765), Johann Baptist Cramer (1771), Joseph Wölfl (1773), and Johann Nepomuk Hummel (1778). Without the financial security of long-term court appointments, most of these men had to support themselves by diversifying their musical activities.[1] It was advantageous for them to live in one of the few large cities whose wealth and cultural life could provide them with lucrative opportunities for teaching and performing: chiefly London, Vienna, and – in its brief periods of political stability – Paris. But there were periods in their lives when they had to lead an itinerant existence, undertaking concert tours throughout Europe. They composed large amounts of piano music, not only as dazzling vehicles for their own virtuosity, but (more profitably) for the amateur market. And many of them became involved in the support industries of their

1

profession: instrument making and music publishing.[2] These virtuosi were thus strategically placed to affect the future developments of the piano and its repertoire. By developing new playing techniques they could expand its musical potential; their involvement with manufacturing firms gave them an influence in the instrument's technical development; and they had the opportunity to shape a new idiomatic style of keyboard music.

It might be trivial, given his historical pre-eminence, to say that Beethoven stands out from his contemporaries. But it is worth stressing that in many ways his career as a pianist-composer was not typical. For most of the 1790s his financial security was guaranteed by a small but powerful group of Viennese aristocratic sponsors, and this protected him from the mass-market forces that weighed heavily upon his leading rivals. After tours to Berlin, Prague and Pressburg in 1796 he was relieved of the need to make extensive foreign journeys, and he was the only major keyboard player of his time never to set foot in Paris or London. Unlike pianists working in London, Beethoven rarely played in large public spaces.[3] His performances were largely confined to Vienna's most elite aristocratic salons where, since the death of Mozart in 1791, the select audiences had become increasingly receptive to high musical seriousness.[4] Among his principal patrons, Baron Gottfried van Swieten and Prince Karl Lichnowsky had a taste for 'learned' serious music that was at odds with more widespread popular tastes. They encouraged Beethoven to pursue his already marked bent towards novel, difficult, and densely-argued music. Uniquely, the circles within which Beethoven worked were socially *and* artistically exclusive. He had no significant contact with the larger musical public and, free from the need to be a popular composer, he could afford largely to eschew middlebrow mass-market values in his performances and compositions.

Technique and technology

Throughout the eighteenth century instrumentalists regarded performance as a rhetorical act. The ideal of affective eloquence was repeatedly stressed in treatises: a fundamental principle was to play as though one were 'speaking in tones', and public performance was likened to oratory. Beethoven seems to have subscribed to this oratorical approach, but he put it into practice in novel ways.[5] Contemporary commentators unanimously recognised fundamental differences between his playing style and those of his leading Viennese rivals.[6] Since the early 1780s, when Mozart had been the dominant virtuoso in Vienna, a highly articulated non-legato style had been considered exemplary. It was characterised by faultless technical ease, a light touch, the smooth production of an even and brilliant 'perlé' tone in rapid passagework, the subtle inflection of melodic lines imitating the ideal of vocal delivery, and the controlled poise with which the player addressed the keyboard. Above all, a good balance should be struck between taste (*Geschmack*) and feeling (*Empfindung*). During the 1790s this style was perpetuated in Vienna by older figures such as Joseph Gelinek (1758–1825) and by rivals from Beethoven's own generation like Hummel and Wölfl, both of whom had personal contacts with Mozart. In contrast, Beethoven is reported to have performed with a more pronounced finger legato, and to have used the undampened resonance of his instruments with less discrimination than his rivals. He played more forcefully than exponents of the older style, but his passagework was sometimes comparatively untidy and he lacked the poise and grace that were the hallmarks of performances by Wölfl and Hummel. His tonal range was wider, but it was perceived to be used with more brutality: consequently accents and sudden changes in dymanics appeared more exaggerated.[7]

Beethoven's individual style was potentially a strong asset in the development of his reputation as a piano virtuoso, since it was evidently well suited to the rhetorical ferocity and expressive intensity of his improvisations. Yet while many commentators were struck by the affective power of his playing, they did not necessarily value other aspects of its originality. During his first decade in Vienna it was in fact more likely to be cited to his detriment than to his advantage.[8] Such negative critiques were brilliantly distilled in Andreas Streicher's vignettes of two (anonymous) pianists in his *Kurze Bemerkungen über das Spielen, Stimmen und Erhalten der Fortepiano* ('Brief Remarks on the Playing, Tuning and Maintainance of the Fortepiano').[9] Streicher gives a detailed account of the older style of playing, whose representative is described as 'a true musician' who has 'learned to subordinate his feelings to the limits of the instrument' so that he is able to 'make us feel what he himself feels'. [10] His second portrait – which, by comparison, reads like a caricature – is of a pianist 'unworthy of imitation':

> A player, of whom it is said 'He plays extraordinarily, like you have never heard before', sits down (or rather throws himself) at the fortepiano. Already the first chords will have been played with such violence ['*Starke*'] that you wonder whether the player is deaf . . . Through the movement of his body, arms and hands, he seemingly wants to make us understand how difficult is the work he has undertaken. He carries on in a fiery manner and treats his instrument like a man who, bent on revenge, has his arch-enemy in his hands and, with cruel relish, wants to torture him slowly to death . . . He pounds so much that suddenly the maltreated strings go out of tune, several fly towards bystanders who hurriedly move back in order to protect their eyes . . . Puff! What was that? He raised the dampers . . . Now he wants to imitate the glass harmonica, but he makes only harsh sounds. Consonances and dissonances flow into one another and we hear only a disgusting mixture of tones.
>
> Short notes are shoved with the arm and hand at the same time, making a racket. If the notes should be slurred together, they are blurred, because he never lifts his fingers at the right time. His playing resembles a script which has been smeared before the ink has dried . . . Is this description exaggerated? Certainly not! A hundred instances could be cited in which 'keyboard stranglers' have broken strings in the most beautiful, gentle adagio. [11]

By 1801 such murderous views of Beethoven's playing were becoming more rare, as critics began to perceive his style as an aesthetically legitimate alternative to his rivals' Mozartian non-legato. No doubt this transformation was connected with the growing critical appreciation of his music at this time: when a high value was placed on his works, the performing style that fostered them came to be acceptable, even desirable. These changes in perception were also partly driven by the projection of Beethoven's reputation by his aristocratic sponsors, since the more prestige he acquired, the less cachet there was in denigrating his manner of performance.

Aesthetic debates generated by this bifurcation in playing styles also affected the directions in which the instruments themselves evolved at the beginning of the nineteenth century. [12] Of course, there was a dynamic and complex relationship between developing keyboard technologies, changing performing techniques, and the demands made by new music. But it can be claimed that Beethoven's ideals, together with the style of his music and playing, had a decisive effect on piano construction in Vienna between 1800 and 1810. In the classical period there were basically two different types of piano mechanism.[13] On the one hand, instruments made in south Germany and Vienna were suited to Mozartian non-legato styles: they had a shallow touch, a light action, and very effective dampers; their sound was delicate, but its qualities varied greatly between registral extremes. English instruments, on the other hand, were better suited to a more sonorous legato style: with a heavier action, they were louder, more resonant, and had greater timbral homogeneity than their Viennese counterparts. At the time Beethoven wrote his Op. 27 and Op. 31 sonatas the latest English pianos were known in Vienna only by repute, and his first-hand knowledge was confined to local instruments. He had been impressed by Johann Andreas Stein's fortepianos in 1787, and in Vienna he kept in close touch with the firm 'Nannette Streicher, geburt Stein', which was run by Stein's daughter and son-in-law. For short periods he seems also to have played pianos by Mozart's preferred maker Anton Walter (*c.* 1801) and by Johann Jakesch (*c.* 1802).[14] But such instruments did not flatter Beethoven's manner of performing, nor did he allow them to fetter his compositional imagination, and there was a significant gap between the capabilities of the instruments available to him and his ideal conception of what a piano ought to be. His dissatisfaction applied particularly to the limitations of the prevalent five-octave range ($FF\text{--}f^3$), the absence of *una corda* mechanisms, and above all the dynamic power and timbral qualities of Viennese instruments.[15] In 1796 he expressed his reservations trenchantly in two well-known letters to Andreas Streicher. Writing from Pressburg, he thanked Streicher for the receipt of a piano, but he joked that it was 'far too good' for him because it 'robs me of the freedom to produce my own tone'.[16] Later in the year he elaborated on the topic:

> There is no doubt that so far as the manner of playing is concerned, the piano is still the least studied and developed of all instruments; often one thinks that one is merely listening to a harp. And I am delighted, my dear fellow, that you are one of the few who realize and perceive that, provided one can feel the music, one can make the piano sing. I hope that the time will come when the harp and the fortepiano will be treated as two entirely different instruments.[17]

What he wanted, then, was more resonant instruments that could cope with his dynamic extremes (especially his strong *forte*) and facilitate his legato-style expressivity. If the comments in Streicher's *Bemerkungen* are anything to go by, he was at that stage hardly sympathetic to Beethoven's aesthetics. But as the composer's reputation and influence grew in the first decade of the nineteenth century, Streicher came under increasing pressure to produce instruments that took account of Beethoven's ideals. Alongside 'classic' Viennese models, his firm started to produce triple-strung pianos with heavier actions, a bigger tone, and an *una corda* mechanism. In DeNora's words, 'Pro-Beethoven values had been partially worked into the very hardware and into the means of musical production itself.'[18]

Music for connoisseurs

Traditional distinctions between keyboard music for connoisseurs and amateurs became more pronounced during the 1790s. Pieces written for amateur performers were technically undemanding, with unadventurous diatonic harmonies, light textures, easily-grasped forms, and simple melodic styles. Certain genres were associated almost exclusively with this market: dances, song arrangements, simple decorative variations or pot-pourri fantasias on popular songs or arias, and descriptive pieces that often played on significant events in current affairs, such as Dussek's *The Sufferings of the Queen of France* (1793). Meanwhile, the music that professionals wrote for themselves to play made increasingly flamboyant technical and musical demands. Two subcategories can be distinguished here. Virtuoso pieces like Dussek's programmatic sonata *The Naval Battle and Total Defeat of the Grand Dutch Fleet by Admiral Duncan on the 11th of October 1797* and Steibelt's *La journée d'Ulm* were targeted at the tastes of non-connoisseur audiences, though they were well beyond the capabilities of all but the best amateur pianists. But a tiny minority of pieces demanding professional executors was designed to appeal to connoisseurs: these included highbrow genres such as preludes and fugues, and free fantasies in the tradition of the north German *Empfindsamer Stil* (the style playing on the audience's sensibilities).

The only genre that bridged all sectors of this culture was the sonata.[19] In terms of quantity, the market was dominated by sonatas written for the domestic use of amateurs: pieces that shared the modest dimensions and facile characteristics of other mass-market genres. Most were written by historically insignificant figures, though even the greatest virtuosi also wrote for players with modest abilities. Mozart described his C major Sonata K.545 (1788) as 'for beginners', Clementi's six sonatinas Op. 36 (1797) proved popular with amateurs, and Beethoven's two sonatas Op. 49 (dating from the mid-1790s) were also composed in this tradition. As far as quality is concerned, however, the repertoire was dominated by a small minority of sonatas that virtuoso pianist-composers wrote for professional players and connoisseurs. It goes without saying that Beethoven's sonatas stand at the pinnacle of this category, but the gulf between the amateur and connoisseur sonatas of his greatest contemporaries is just as wide as the gap between Beethoven's Op. 49 and, for example, the 'Pathétique'.

A number of historians have explored similarities between Beethoven's keyboard music and sonatas by Clementi, Dussek, Cramer and George Frederick Pinto (1785–1806), composers of the so-called 'London Pianoforte School'.[20] Anyone who has heard 'professional' sonatas by these composers cannot fail to have noticed turns of phrase, textures, colourful harmonic progressions and formal strategies that are reminiscent of Beethoven. He undoubtedly knew some of the music emanating from London and, when specific comparisons can be drawn between a Beethoven sonata and a 'London' sonata, chronology usually gives precedence to the latter. But artistic influence is a problematic and elusive concept; even if historians could establish that conditions at the time made an exchange of ideas possible, two fundamental problems would remain. First, the concept of the 'musical idea' embraces such a wide range of possibilities – from the shortest motive to the most intangible generalities about form, rhetoric and style – that it might not be easy to categorise the raw materials of the exchange. Second, even if Beethoven had taken on board ideas from the London composers, it might be difficult to identify with any confidence the trace they leave in his music; indeed, the more he assimilated an idea, the harder it would be to identify the source of the influence at all. With this in mind, it is perhaps preferable to speak of stylistic *affinities* between Beethoven and these contemporaries, affinities which can be claimed most plausibly on the largest scale:

1 Sonatas increasingly acquired symphonic characteristics. They were in the 'Grand' style, with imposing ideas, rich textures, brilliant figuration, and broad structures. Individual movements grew in size, and sonatas sometimes contained four movements rather than the classical norm of three.

2 Greater demands were made on the technique of the performer and the technical capabilities of the instrument.

3 There was a tendency for composers to establish a stylistic distance between their sonatas and classical models. This could take many forms, such as the deformation of normative sonata-form processes, the ironic treatment of classical clichés, the exploration of mediant tonal relationships and of keys related chromatically to the tonic, the avoidance of regular periodic phrase structures, the inclusion of popular elements like song themes in slow movements and variation finales, or an increased emphasis on virtuosity for its own sake.

Despite these common features, the greater density, cogency, energy, and above all, the more imaginative daring of Beethoven's music is inevitably striking. Just as his playing attracted opprobrium in the 1790s, so his sonatas were variously described as being 'overladen with difficulties', 'strange', 'obstinate', and 'unnatural'.[21] Beethoven's pursuit of these anti-popular characteristics in his music can, of course, be attributed to the unique nature of his musical talents and his highly individual artistic personality; but it can also be traced back to the supportive environment of the elite salons in Vienna.

An important new phenomenon emerged in the musical culture of both London and Vienna at the end of the eighteenth century. In the face of a mainstream preoccupation with the new and contemporary, musical connoisseurs became interested in performing old (mostly Baroque) music and perpetuating its values. The preservation of non-contemporary repertoires may be viewed as the first step towards the creation of a musical canon in the nineteenth century, but it took very different forms in the two cities concerned.[22] 'Ancient' music was kept as a separate category from modern music in London. So while English connoisseurs revered Handel's music, they would not have expected contemporary composers such as Clementi and Dussek to aspire to its sublime 'greatness'. In contrast, Viennese connoisseurs like Gottfried van Swieten seem not to have made such a categorical distinction between the best examples of old and new music. By constructing a tradition of 'great' music that stretched from J. S. Bach and Handel, through C. P. E. Bach, Mozart and Haydn (still at the height of his powers), to embrace Beethoven, van Swieten and his colleagues were creating an appreciative context in which Beethoven could explore musical difficulty to an unprecedented degree.[23]

These elitist tastes illuminate the background to the commission and publication of Beethoven's Op. 31 sonatas by the Zurich music publisher Hans Georg Nägeli. Two of Nägeli's boldest projects reflect the complementary aspects of old and new music which were so significant in the emergence of a Viennese canon. In 1802 he began to issue 'classic' keyboard music from the first half of the eighteenth century, including works by J. S. Bach and Handel, in a series entitled *Musikalische Kunstwerke im strengen Schreibart* ('Musical works in the strict style').[24] And in the following year he started another series with the aim of creating a complementary classic repertoire of contemporary piano music. The *Répertoire des Clavecinistes* was initially envisaged on a vast scale, though eventually only seventeen volumes appeared. Nägeli intended to reprint excellent examples of recent music, and to commission the leading virtuoso-composers. His notion of excellence can be reconstructed from notices that appeared in the musical press in 1803. First he outlined the project's broad aims. Crediting Clementi with the founding of the modern piano style, Nägeli said that he wanted to collect the most excellent examples by the best composers (additionally naming Cramer, Dussek, Steibelt, and Beethoven), so that the competition would spur them on to greater things. The ambitious nature of the enterprise was revealed in a remarkable passage spelling out his aesthetic criteria:

> I am interested mainly in piano solos in the grand style, large in size, and with many departures from the usual form of the sonata. These products should be distinguished by their wealth of detail and full sonorities. Artistic piano figuration must be interwoven with contrapuntal phrases.[25]

Clearly the *Répertoire* was aimed at connoisseurs rather than amateurs, but Nägeli was aware that an emphasis on virtuosity might discourage both parties: amateurs would balk at the technical demands and connoisseurs would disapprove of 'empty' technical virtuosity without serious content. Perhaps it was this inherent commercial danger that prompted Nägeli to highlight the combination of brilliant and serious elements he required:

> It might be displeasing to talk of virtuosity as a principal requirement here. But one should consider that from Clementi onwards all outstanding composers of keyboard music are also excellent virtuosi, and this is undoubtedly the reason for the appeal and liveliness of their products, since it channels their physical and spiritual power in precisely this direction. Therefore such complete artists are rightly held up as models. It goes without saying, then, that compositional thoroughness must not be neglected . . . Those who have no contrapuntal skill and are not piano virtuosi will hardly be able to achieve much here.[26]

With their focus on a mixture of the grand style, formal originality, contrapuntal skill and brilliant figuration, Nägeli's criteria might well have been tailored around Beethoven's keyboard music.

2

Beethoven in 1800–1802

Beethoven was in his early thirties when he wrote the Op. 27 and Op. 31 sonatas. To most observers his life must have seemed sweet at this time. He was working in a stable and increasingly appreciative environment. In 1800 Prince Lichnowsky settled an annuity of 600 gulden on him; his *Akademie* (benefit concert) at the Burgtheater on 2 April 1800 further cemented his position as one of Vienna's leading musicians; and with the prestigious commission and favourable reception of his ballet *Die Geschöpfe des Prometheus* ('The Creatures of Prometheus') Op. 43 he scored his first big public success. Foreign music publishers were beginning to take an interest in acquiring his works, and reviews in the *Allgemeine musikalische Zeitung* were becoming more positive. This was also a highly productive period. On-going projects such as the Op. 18 string quartets and the third piano concerto (Op. 37) were completed in 1800. The next two years saw the composition of the second symphony (Op. 36), a string quintet (Op. 29), five violin sonatas (Opp. 23, 24 and 30), two sets of piano variations Opp. 34 and 35, and no fewer than seven piano sonatas (Opp. 22, 26, 27, 28 and 31).

But in contrast to the outward trappings of a flourishing career, Beethoven secretly faced personal turmoil as he struggled to come to terms with the onset of deafness. His hearing had begun to deteriorate around 1796–8, and by 1800 he was avoiding social gatherings, fearing that his disability would become common knowledge. He sought medical help, but to no avail. On 29 June 1801 he wrote to the physician Franz Wegeler in Bonn, giving details of his symptoms ('my ears continue to hum and buzz day and night . . . at a distance I cannot hear the high notes of instruments or voices') and describing the treatments to which he had been subjected.[1] Two days later, in a letter to another Bonn friend, Karl Amenda, Beethoven tempered his pessimism with hope. In

11

addition to the revelation of his deafness, he gave Amenda an account of the latest developments in his career, and wrote of plans for future concert tours. It is possible to see the optimism of this letter as evidence of Beethoven's indomitable spirit; though his sudden switches of tone – from self-pity to euphoria – and over-emphatic assurances of future success can also appear desperate, if not manic:

> Oh, how happy should I be now if I had perfect hearing . . . But in my present condition I must withdraw from everything; and my best years will rapidly pass away without my being able to achieve all that my talent and strength have commanded me to do – sad resignation, to which I am forced to have recourse. Needless to say, I am resolved to overcome all this, but how is it going to be done? Yes, Amenda, if after six months my disease proves to be incurable, then I shall claim your sympathy, then you must give up everything and come to me. I shall then travel (when I am playing and composing, my affliction still hampers me least; it affects me most when I am in company) and you must be my companion. I am convinced that my luck will not forsake me. Why, at the moment I feel equal to anything.[2]

Beethoven's hopes of recovery might have seemed well founded in the short term. During the second half of 1801 he appears to have had some remission from his tinnitus. A more calmly optimistic letter to Wegeler on 16 November tells that he was 'leading a slightly more pleasant life, for I am mixing more with my fellow creatures'.[3] The change in mood was not only due to his improved health, but also to 'a dear charming girl who loves me and whom I love': generally taken to be a reference to the sixteen-year-old Countess Giulietta Guicciardi.[4] In his new state of wellbeing, Beethoven even mentioned the possibility of marriage, despite differences in age and background. But in the early months of 1802 he suffered a series of setbacks: his hearing worsened, he failed to obtain permission to use the Burgtheater for a second benefit concert, and it is possible that his assessment of his prospects of marrying the countess became more realistic. He moved from Vienna to the nearby village of Heiligenstadt in the late spring of 1802, perhaps on medical advice, and remained there until the middle of October. His increasing despair during the summer was captured in Ferdinand Ries's famous anecdote about a walk he took with the composer in the Heiligenstadt countryside:

I called his attention to a shepherd in the forest who was playing most pleasantly on a flute cut from lilac wood. For half an hour Beethoven could not hear anything at all and became extremely quiet and gloomy, even though I repeatedly assured him that I did not hear anything any longer either (which was, however, not the case). – When at times he did seem in good spirits, he often became actually boisterous. However, this happened very rarely.[5]

It may have been the prospect of his imminent return to Vienna that prompted Beethoven to take stock of the situation. On 6 October he wrote his brothers a long letter to be made public after his death: an *apologia pro vita sua*, in which he defended himself from the charge of misanthropy, resigned himself to the incurability of his deafness, and explained that only his music had prevented him from suicide. A postscript was added on 10 October, reiterating his resignation. It was discovered among Beethoven's papers in 1827.[6]

The Heiligenstadt Testament has been seen by many of Beethoven's biographers as a signal document: the record of a cathartic moment in his inner life which had profound consequences for his creativity. Thus for Roman Rolland 'it was precisely at this moment that the demon of the *Eroica* cried out within him "Forward!"'.[7] Rolland perceived Beethoven's deafness not so much as an obstacle to be overcome, but as an infirmity that was paradoxically enabling: 'Beethoven's genius (I ought to say his "demon") produced his deafness. Did not the deafness, in its turn, make the genius, or at all events aid it?'[8] Similarly, Maynard Solomon views the Testament as 'a leave-taking – which is to say, a fresh start. Beethoven here enacted his own death in order that he might live again. He recreated himself in a new guise, self-sufficient and heroic.' Solomon, too, explores the possibility that Beethoven's deafness may have played a positive role in his creativity, freeing him from the distractions and rigidities of the material world. Once again invoking heroic metaphors, he argues that the creative role of Beethoven's deafness transcended mere utility, because 'all of Beethoven's defeats were, ultimately, turned into victories . . . even his loss of hearing was in some obscure way necessary (or at least useful) to the fulfilment of his creative quest. The onset of deafness was the painful chrysalis within which his "heroic" style came to maturity.'[9]

Such views rest on the assumption that aspects of a composer's life must inform his music, so that a reading of the life should parallel a reading of the works in a mutually supporting framework. How far, though, can such parallels be drawn? Perhaps those who subscribe to this position might feel obliged to look for confessional works that are contemporary with, and mirror the letters to Amenda, Wegeler, and Beethoven's brothers. They need not be put off by the lack of overtly programmatic music, since Beethoven evidently wanted his deafness to remain a secret from his Viennese patrons. Where better to look for a covert programme than in the heightened subjectivity of a fantasy, or – failing that – a sonata *quasi una fantasia*? Perhaps the 'Moonlight' Sonata is not, after all, an expression of Beethoven's sorrow at losing Giulietta Guicciardi: the claim, though made often enough, has absolutely nothing to recommend it from a biographical perspective. A far more precious loss to Beethoven at that time was his hearing. Why are the dynamics of the sonata's first movement unprecedentedly suppressed to a constant *piano* or softer? Why does the melody emerge from, and resubmerge into, an under-articulated accompanimental continuum? Why is the movement centred on low sonorities, and the extreme treble reached only once, in a gesture of the utmost despair? Perhaps this is a representation of Beethoven's impaired auditory world, and – at the same time – a lament for his loss. Why does the sonata's Presto agitato finale seem to cover the same ground as the first movement, but with a prevailing mood of manic rage, rather than of melancholy? Perhaps the contrast reflects the two significant states of mind that emerge from Beethoven's letters at the time.

It is all too easy to let such speculation run wild. Given the evident interpretational dangers in holding this position, a cautious approach to . apparent relationships between life and works is always called for. As one critic has warned: 'In our own, demythologizing times . . . the relation of art to life seems altogether too simple'.[10] The fact that Beethoven, like many early nineteenth-century writers and artists, did occasionally write confessional pieces (for example, the *Heiliger Dankgesang* from the String Quartet Op. 132) gives historians no automatic licence to assume that all works have covert autobiographical elements. On the evidence of the sources, it seems that Beethoven had periods of anxiety and other periods of relative contentment during this time. His anxiety stemmed not so much from the problems caused by his deafness, as from his fears about its future course. He did not know how soon his successful career would be curtailed, either through infirmity, or through the machinations of his enemies. But his worries seem to have been focused on his social life, rather than his musical life: in his own words, 'Thanks . . . to my art, I did not end my life by suicide.'[11] The sentiments expressed in the Heiligenstadt Testament were anticipated to some extent in the earlier letters to Wegeler and Amenda. Rather than representing a turning point – a new breakthrough in his acceptance of his condition – the document may been seen as containing a crystallisation of thoughts that Beethoven had been exploring for some time.

Yet there is anecdotal evidence that Beethoven was planning to take his music in new directions. According to Czerny, around the time he finished the Op. 28 sonata (1801, though Czerny dates it 1800), Beethoven expressed some dissatisfaction with his previous pieces, and declared that henceforth he was determined to 'take a new path'.[12] For Czerny, writing in 1838, this new path was exemplified by the Op. 31 sonatas. Similarly, only days after returning to Vienna from Heiligenstadt in October 1802, Beethoven wrote to the Leipzig publishers Breitkopf and Härtel about two new sets of piano variations (Opp. 34 and 35) which he had composed 'in quite a *new manner*, and each in a *separate and different way*'.[13] With historical hindsight, it is clear that Beethoven was on the verge of forging a radically new style in 1802; but it cannot be claimed that the works of 1801–2 themselves represent such a clear break with the past. Instead, as with the relationship between the Heiligenstadt Testament and the 1801 letters, it is possible to view the innovative aspects of Op. 27 and Op. 31 as an unprecedented focusing of several features of Beethoven's style that had been emerging gradually during the 1790s.

First, there was an increased element of fantasy: musical gestures became more markedly personal; forms were shaped as much by the idiosyncrasies of their unique contents as by an adherence to traditional models; and the coherence of multi-movement works was intensified by the use of recurrent unifying basic ideas from movement to movement. Douglas Johnson has drawn attention to the 'substitution of organic processes for mechanical ones within, and to a limited extent between, movements' in certain pieces from the mid-1790s.[14] He shows how motivic details can affect larger aspects of form, including tonal patterns.

While Beethoven's earlier experiments in this direction largely affected the tonal course of development sections, towards 1802 he began to extend the principle to other areas of sonata form, areas traditionally more prescribed by tonal conventions. In the first movment of the String Quintet Op. 29 (1802), for example, Beethoven's development of the opening theme's semitone motive has profound consequences for the key of the exposition's second subject, which appears in bar 41 in the highly unconventional submediant major (A major).

However, it was in the slow movements of his earlier sonatas, especially those not in sonata form, that Beethoven gave most free rein to his fantasy, and in which fantastic elements are most integral to the shape of the music. Outstanding amongst these is the Largo e mesto from the Sonata in D Op. 10 no. 3 (1797–8), whose harmonic richness, gestural strangeness, and motivic-formal complexities have long made it a favourite with critics and analysts as well as performers. Beethoven's tendency to highlight the fantastic element in his music was taken further by strategically placing a slow movement (a set of variations) instead of a conventional sonata allegro at the start of the Sonata in A♭ Op. 26 (1800). But it was not until the Op. 27 sonatas that he explored the implications of combining all these features: starting with a slow fantasy-like movement, and forging strong links between movements.

Related to these techniques was the way in which Beethoven increasingly focused the long-term goal-orientation of his music by exploring the consequences of unstable ideas at the start of movements. Of course, this strategy was not without precedent: there are many well-known examples of off-tonic openings and bizarre introductory gestures in the music of Carl Philipp Emanuel Bach and Joseph Haydn.[15] But the novelty in this aspect of Beethoven's style lies in his single-minded pursuit of the consequences of unstable openings, and the power and clarity of the results. His interest in unstable openings increased markedly around the turn of the century. Examples from the years leading up to Op. 31 are the opening of the First Symphony (Op. 21; 1799–1800), the second movement Menuetto from the Sonata Op. 26 (1801–2), and the fourth movement of the C minor Violin Sonata Op. 30 no. 2 (1802).

If, by the time he came to write the Op. 31 sonatas, Beethoven had not yet found the economy of the Eroica's famous c♯, he was nevertheless able to pursue the implications of initial harmonic instability and motivic pregnancy more thoroughly and on a wider scale than in any of his earlier works. Beethoven's innovations were advancing on all fronts at this stage in his career; but, as Nicholas Marston has observed, he 'appears to have preferred the intimate medium of the piano for the mould-breaking works' of 1802.[16]

3

Composition and reception

The composition of Op. 27 and Op. 31

During the first three months of 1801 Beethoven was preoccupied with the composition of the ballet *Die Geschöpfe des Prometheus* Op. 43, which had been commissioned – probably at some time during the second half of 1800 – for performance at the Imperial Court Theatre.[1] At the same time, he continued to work intermittently on another commission, the Sonata for violin and piano in F Op. 24 ('Spring') for Count Moritz von Fries, and on the Piano Sonata in A♭ Op. 26. Sketches for these pieces dominate the last half of Landsberg 7, the sketchbook that Beethoven used between the summer of 1800 and the spring of 1801.[2] Additionally, there are a few brief sketches for other works in this part of Landsberg 7: one for the Bagatelle Op. 33 no. 7, and – on bifolia that also contain ideas for the ballet and Op. 26 – a small group of concept sketches for the E♭ Sonata Op. 27 no. 1.[3] Perhaps too much could be made of the fact that the earliest notated ideas for the first *quasi una fantasia* sonata date from the time when Beethoven was primarily thinking about ballet. But several parallels can be drawn between *Prometheus* and the sonata's fantasy characteristics. First, the ballet's narrative structure prompted Beethoven to avoid using sonata form after the overture, and to treat other normative forms in unconventional ways. His experience of writing *Prometheus* must have suggested how these principles could be transferred to other genres, such as the sonata, whose formal patterns were more bound by convention. Second, there are many *attacca* indications between movements in the ballet and in the sonata, and a concern for the tension between discrete formal units and broader stretches of musical continuity is evident in both works. Third, the ballet and sonata share some detailed characteristics: sudden and extreme changes of tempo, cadenza-like gestures, and closing sections (both in E♭) in the style of comic opera finales.

There is no evidence that Beethoven was commissioned to write the Op. 27 sonatas, and it seems likely that in the spring of 1801 he finished work on his commissions before moving on to pieces that he was writing for himself. At any rate, the content of Landsberg 7 suggests that Beethoven did not begin sustained work on Op. 27 until after the premiere of *Prometheus* on 28 March 1801. Given the relatively extensive sketches for Op. 24 and Op. 26 in Landsberg 7, he may well have finished these sonatas in the aftermath of the ballet, delaying work on Op. 27 still later into 1801. Unfortunately it is impossible to verify this hypothesis, due to the large gaps in the sources for music that Beethoven composed between April and December 1801. During this eight-month period he probably used a single book for his sketches, now known as the Sauer Sketchbook after the Viennese music dealer who purchased it at the auction of Beethoven's effects in 1827.[4] Sauer seems to have sold individual leaves from the book to souvenir hunters and, although it may originally have contained around ninety-six leaves, only twenty-two of them have been positively identified, scattered in various collections throughout the world.[5] Five of these extant leaves contain sketches for the finale of the C♯ minor Sonata Op. 27 no. 2, and the other seventeen are filled with work on the Sonata in D Op. 28 and the first three movements of the String Quintet Op. 29. Johnson, Tyson and Winter cautiously suggest that the surviving leaves may represent an almost complete torso from the middle of the sketchbook, rather than a random series of leaves from various parts of the original source,[6] in which case, complete sections from the beginning and end of the book are lost. It is possible that sketches for the other movements of the Op. 27 sonatas were entered in some of the leaves from the lost opening section of the sketchbook, but it cannot be established exactly when Beethoven started or finished work on Op. 27. *If* he completed Op. 27 before moving on to the D major Sonata and the Quintet, and *if* subsequent segments of the Sauer sketchbook are indeed lost, then it seems unlikely that work on the fantasy-sonatas can have stretched far beyond the early autumn of 1801. Other sources provide no further clues: the sonatas are not mentioned in Beethoven's correspondence around that time; the autograph manuscript of the E♭ Sonata is lost, and that of the C♯ minor Sonata is lacking its first and last leaves, that is, the very pages that Beethoven is most likely to have dated; and no *Stichvorlagen* (clean copies prepared for the publisher) are known.

The sonatas were published in March 1802 by Giovanni Cappi in Vienna, shortly followed by another edition from Nikolaus Simrock in Bonn.[7] Unusually for a set published under a single opus number, they carried individual dedications: the E♭ Sonata to Princess Josephine von Liechtenstein, and the C♯ minor Sonata to Countess Giulietta Guicciardi. Both ladies frequented the Viennese salons in which Beethoven was lionised at that time: the princess was a relative of Beethoven's Bonn patron Count Ferdinand von Waldstein, and the countess was a member of the Brunsvik family, with whom the composer was on close terms in the early 1800s. Although Beethoven may have been in love with Giulietta Guicciardi in 1801, rather too much has been made of the dedication of Op. 27 no. 2. Indeed, there is anecdotal evidence that the dedication – far from signalling that the countess was somehow the inspiration for the work – was incidental, if not accidental. In conversation with Otto Jahn in 1852, Countess Gallenberg (as Giulietta became on her marriage in 1803) reported that Beethoven had initially intended to dedicate to her the Rondo in G Op. 51 no. 2. But, finding that he needed something suitable to give to Prince Karl Lichnowsky's sister Henriette, he asked Giulietta to return the Rondo, and (with the implication that it was a consolation prize?) later gave her the C♯ minor Sonata instead.[8]

It was probably only a few weeks after the publication of the Op. 27 sonatas that Beethoven received a commission for three piano sonatas from Hans Georg Nägeli.[9] In the late spring of 1802 the composer was already in Heiligenstadt putting the finishing touches to the three sonatas for violin and piano Op. 30. On 22 April Beethoven's brother Carl – who at this time negotiated the sale of the composer's works to publishers – wrote to the Leipzig music publishers Breitkopf and Härtel:

> By and by we shall determine for you the prices for other pieces of music and after we are of one mind on them, every time that we have a piece it will be delivered to the financial agent whom you specify to us: for example – 50 ducats for a grand sonata for the piano, 130 ducats for three sonatas with or without accompaniment. At present we have three sonatas for the piano and violin, and if they please you, then we shall send them.[10]

His reference to 'three sonatas . . . without accompaniment' is tantalising. Was it pure speculation about possible future projects? Was Beethoven already planning to write some piano sonatas during the summer of 1802, before he received Nägeli's commission? Or had the composer already received and accepted Nägeli's request? It is possible that Carl van Beethoven was already laying the groundwork to entice Breitkopf and Härtel into buying the sonatas for a higher price than Nägeli had offered. Six weeks later, on 1 June, he again wrote to Breitkopf, reminding him of the earlier letter 'concerning piano sonatas'. Again this reference is ambiguous: was he now referring more openly to Op. 31, or is 'piano sonatas' shorthand for 'piano sonatas with violin accompaniment'? If Beethoven had made progress in his work on the piano sonatas by this date, then his brother would have felt able to make a firmer proposal to the publisher. As it happened, the negotiations quickly came to nothing. In replies on 8 and 10 June, Breitkopf rejected Carl's prices, saying that pirated editions would prevent the firm from recouping such large costs.[11] Nevertheless, Beethoven's brother continued with his machinations. A draft letter from Nägeli to his Paris business associate Johann Jakob Horner, dated 18 July 1802, mentions a letter he had just received from Carl:

> He counsels me in a friendly way . . . that I should enclose with my reply a letter to his brother, with the request that he reduce the price somewhat. His brother does not have so much business sense, and so he will perhaps do it. Now I am resolved to send him, by the post that leaves today, a bill of exchange that will bring the total (with that already sent) to 100 ducats, and instead of a reduction in price, ask him for a fourth sonata into the deal.
>
> Then we [shall] have two Beethoven issues for the *Répertoire*. I am therefore also determined to make it so, whereby I am sure to receive at least the three sonatas in any case by the next post, and can send them to you in Paris. After a more accurate reckoning, these sonatas can arrive by the post coach of 17 August, and can be sent to you on the 19th, and arrive in Paris about 1 September. At most a week later.[12]

No doubt Carl's confidential advice to Nägeli, that he reduce the price of the sonatas, was calculated to provoke Beethoven into breaking off his agreement, thereby allowing Carl to sell the sonatas elsewhere for a higher price. In the event it was the brothers who quarrelled, and when the three sonatas that had been originally commissioned were finally ready to be dispatched to Zurich, the composer entrusted the task to his young pupil Ferdinand Ries. According to Ries this happened before Beethoven left Heiligenstadt in the middle of October, though it is unlikely to have occurred as early as Nägeli was evidently expecting.[13] Commentators have offered differing views on whether the evidence of the sketches supports Ries's account. Johnson, Tyson and Winter argue that if Beethoven had waited for the misunderstandings in Nägeli's letter of 18 July to be cleared up, then he might not have begun serious work on the sonatas until July or even August 1802; it follows that he would not have begun using the Wielhorsky sketchbook until late September or early October, and it is highly unlikely that he would have completed neat copies of all three sonatas in time to send them to Zurich before he returned to Vienna.[14] Albrecht, on the other hand, has reconsidered the chronology of Wielhorsky by working backwards from the later sketches for *Christus am Ölberge*, a method that is not without risk, given the variable rate at which Beethoven worked. He suggests that the composer might have entered the sketches for Op. 31 no. 3 on the first eleven pages of Wielhorsky as early as August, and certainly not later than the middle of September 1802.[15] While it is impossible to verify this hypothesis, it is perhaps worth asking why Ries's account should be doubted at all. Despite occasional memory lapses and misremembered dates in the *Biographische Notizen*, Ries had nothing to gain by deliberately falsifying his role in the events of 1802, and nothing in the sources can be shown to contradict his version of events.

Manuscript copies of the sonatas may have been made available to some of Beethoven's staunchest patrons in Vienna in the autumn of 1802. On 12 November Countess Josephine Deym wrote to a relative: 'I have new sonatas by Beethoven which surpass [literally 'annihilate', *vernichten*] all previous ones.'[16] Nägeli was not ready to issue the Op. 31 sonatas until May 1803, when nos. 1 and 2 appeared as series 5 of the *Répertoire des Clavecinistes*.[17] Presumably the E♭ Sonata was held back because Nägeli was still at that stage hoping to secure a fourth sonata from Beethoven. Notoriously, Nägeli went ahead with the publication of nos. 1 and 2 without allowing the composer to see any proofs. Ries gave a colourful account of the scene when Beethoven finally received a copy:

Example 3.1 Nageli's addition to the first edition of Op. 31 no. 1

When the proofs arrived, I found Beethoven busy writing. 'Play the sonatas through for me', he said, while he remained sitting at his writing desk. There was an uncommon number of mistakes in the proofs, which made Beethoven very impatient indeed. At the end of the first Allegro in the Sonata in G major, however, Nägeli had even included four measures of his own composition, after the fourth beat of the last fermata [see Example 3.1]. When I played these, Beethoven jumped up in a rage, ran over, and all but pushed me from the piano, shouting: 'Where the devil does it say that?' – His astonishment and anger can hardly be imagined when he saw it printed that way. I was told to draw up a list of all the errors and to send the sonatas to Simrock in Bonn who was to reprint them and add, *Edition très correcte*.[18]

Clearly Beethoven felt that drastic action was needed if he was to save his reputation from this disaster. On 21 May 1803 his brother Carl wrote to Breitkopf and Härtel: 'be so good as to announce provisionally in your *Zeitung* that, through an oversight, the Sonatas of Beethoven that have just appeared in Zurich were distributed without corrections, and therefore still contain many errors. I shall send you a list of errors in a few days, so that you can also announce them'.[19] Four days later he wrote to Simrock: 'If you want to reprint the sonatas that appeared in Zurich, write to us and we shall send you a list of some 80 errors in them.'[20] In response to the letter of 23 May, Härtel wrote to the composer on 2 June that the *Allgemeine musikalische Zeitung* would announce the list of corrections to the first two sonatas.[21] On 29 June Ries sent the list of errors and a *Stichvorlage* of the sonatas to Simrock,[22] and in a further letter on 6 August Ries told Simrock that 'the third [sonata] will shortly be issued; Nägeli wanted to have one more sonata, which he will not get, however, because Beethoven is now writing two symphonies, one of which is practically finished'.[23] The proofs of Simrock's edition reached

Beethoven after 13 September;[24] on 22 October Ries sent Simrock a list of errors in the 'corrected' edition, and on 11 December – after Simrock's edition had appeared – he forwarded yet another correction to the bass at bars 200–205 in the finale of the G major Sonata.[25] Giovanni Cappi also issued the G major and D minor Sonatas as Op. 29 in Vienna during the autumn of 1802.[26] Nägeli never received his fourth work, and the E♭ Sonata was paired with a reprint of the *Sonate pathétique* Op. 13 when it appeared as series 11 of the *Répertoire* in the autumn of 1804.[27] Around the same time Simrock and Cappi also published editions of the third sonata, so that the integrity of the set that had occupied Beethoven during the summer of 1802 was finally re-established in print after some two years.

Sketches

A thorough description of the sketches for Op. 27 and Op. 31 lies beyond the scope of this book; nor can the complex and subtle relationships between sketches and 'finished' works be explored in detail here. Instead, the following paragraphs highlight particularly striking aspects of Beethoven's preparatory work on the sonatas. By 1802 the composer's habit of sketching his music before writing out an autograph score had settled into fairly stable patterns. Scholars have identified four basic types of sketches in the sketchbooks of this period, categorised according to their different functions in the development of a work. Though not exhaustive, nor always as clear-cut in practice as in theory, these categories do, however, give a good indication of the route from initial ideas to autograph score.

1. The sketching process usually began with a series of *concept sketches*, which contain 'the germ of an idea'.[28] These are often no more than a few bars long, attempting to fix an initial or subsequent idea for a movement. Such sketches survive for parts of Op. 27 no. 1 and all three Op. 31 sonatas.[29]

2. More rarely Beethoven made a *synopsis sketch* of a movement before beginning more detailed work. This was a sketch outlining the main features of the entire movement, giving brief (and often gnomic) indications of, for example, the thematic running order, significant formal moments (such as the joins between exposition and develop-

ment), and changes of key, tempo, or metre. In the Kessler sketchbook there are synopsis sketches for the second movement of Op. 31 no. 1 (see below, p. 30) and the first movement of Op. 31 no. 2.[30]

3. Next Beethoven tended to sketch large stretches of a movement, so that its broad formal outline and general proportions could be established: these have been termed *continuity sketches*.[31] Not all the details are present at this stage: often the sketch is contained on single staves rather than two-stave systems, and only the *Hauptstimme* is given. In general, harmonies are only indicated as mnemonics at strategic points, and – conversely – sometimes only a harmonic outline is notated without an indication of the motivic material that will eventually clothe it; but in complex contrapuntal passages, Beethoven usually notates all the parts in more detail. There are continuity sketches for the Finale of Op. 27 no. 2 on some of the surviving Sauer leaves, for the first and second movements of Op. 31 no. 1 in Kessler, and for the first, third, and fourth movements of Op. 31 no. 3 in Wielhorsky.

4. In the final stages of sketching it often seems as though Beethoven's compositional process advanced through the dialectical interplay of continuity sketches and *variants*.[32] These vary in length and can accomplish any number of tasks, but they all have the general function of providing alternatives to, or elaborations of, concept sketches and passages from the continuity sketches. In this way Beethoven often built up complex networks between any number of sketches so that, for example, there might be multiple variants that explore alternatives to a 'parent' variant which in turn had elaborated the skeletal area of a continuity sketch. Sometimes, as with the second movement of Op. 31 no. 3, the variants became so convoluted that Beethoven redrafted the entire continuity sketch.[33] All the movements listed under (3) above have copious variants.

Too few sketches survive to cast much light on the genesis of the Op. 27 sonatas, and – given the problematic fragmentary nature of the Sauer sketchbook – any comments on the sketchleaves of the C♯minor Sonata's finale must be highly speculative. Nevertheless there are some intriguing pointers to the ways in which Beethoven's conception of the movement evolved. Two early synopsis sketches for the finale on f.1 of Sauer suggest that Beethoven had already worked out the shape of the exposition in broad terms: skeletal versions of the first and second subjects are

Table 3.1. Sources of sketches for Op. 27 and Op. 31

Landsberg 7 (SPK)	f. 52	Op. 27/1/i Allegro
	f. 69	Op. 27/1/i, ii, iv
Sauer (various collections)[34]	f. 1–5	Op. 27/2/iii
Kessler (Bonn, Bh)	f. 88r, f. 91v–96v	Op. 31/1
	f. 65v, f. 90v	Op. 31/2[35]
	f. 93r, f. 95v	Op. 31/3/i?
Wielhorsky (Moscow, CMMC)	pp. 1–11	Op. 31/3/i, ii, iv

already in place (f.1r staves 1–12); although the final version's third theme (bars 43 to 56) is missing, the exposition's closing theme – marked 'Schluß' above the first bar – appears in a more expansive form than in the sonata on staves 1–6 of f. 1v. There are numerous differences in detail between these early sketches and later versions of the themes, some particularly telling. The opening theme is notated in continous semiquaver figuration like a *moto perpetuo*, without the final version's arresting $g\sharp^2$ quavers at the end of bars 2 and 4. Its accompanimental quavers circumscribe smaller intervals than in later versions: C$\sharp$/E (bars 1–2), B$\sharp^1$/D$\sharp$ (bars 2–4), B$\natural^1$/E$\sharp$ (bars 5–6), A^1/F$\sharp$ (bars 7–8). When the head-motive returns at bar 16 the bass line is an octave lower than in the sonata, moving from C$\sharp$ through A$\sharp^1$ to F$_x^1$. On the fortepianos of Beethoven's day such writing would surely have sounded as much like an inarticulate growl as a functional harmonic progression. And, although Beethoven may have transposed the bass to a higher octave for structural reasons, it is tempting to believe that he was also shying away from the sketch's more brutal sonorities.

While the basic outline of the second subject (its melodic shape G$\sharp$–F$_x$–G$\sharp$–A$\sharp$–B) is present in this concept sketch, it lacks several of the final version's components: the upper-note appoggiaturas at the start of every bar, the constant reiteration of d$\sharp^2$, the second phrase's higher octave and syncopated rhythms, and the chromatic interruption of its cadential formula with b$\sharp^2$ (bar 29). A particularly striking feature of this sketch is the close relationship between the second subject and the exposition's closing theme (see Example 3.2), a similarity that was disguised in Beethoven's subsequent work on them. In these early versions both themes are built from repeated four-bar units, and the derivation of one

Example 3.2 Sauer Sketchleaves (a). f. 1r stave 9 bars 1–4

(b). f. 1v stave 1 bars 1–4

(a).

(b). Schluss

from the other is clear: the second subject's head-motive is displaced by two bars in the 'Schluß' theme. Perhaps Beethoven found the similarity between them too obvious and the pace of the closing theme too leisurely. Later versions of the closing idea compress its constituent elements into two-bar units by superimposing the second and fourth bars.

Other sketches suggest that the development section and coda were the last parts of the movement to be finalised. Beethoven settled quickly on the harmonic plan and thematic content of the development, using the opening theme to modulate to F♯ minor and the second subject to return to V/c♯ via G major and other keys on the flat side of C♯. But in the sketching process the modulatory part of the development was gradually simplified and shortened, so that in the final version G major appears as a Neapolitan inflection of the underlying F♯ minor; at the same time the dominant pedal leading to the recapitulation grew to fifteen bars in the final version. Before hitting upon the idea of ending the movement with a return to sweeping arpeggios from the opening, Beethoven seems to have tried out several alternative conclusions. A seven-bar sketch on staves 5–6 of f. 3v seems to envisage a return to the sonata's opening triplets in the bass, and a final emphasis on the Neapolitan motive that links the sonata's outer movements (see Example 3.3). Later concept sketches for the end of the movement focus on developments of the third theme, though there are no traces of this theme in the coda of the final version.

Surviving sources related to the composition of Op. 31, though not complete, are more substantial than material for Op. 27. There are

Example 3.3 Sauer Sketchleaves f. 3v staves 5–7

copious sketches for the first two movements of the G major Sonata at
the end of the Kessler sketchbook, and for the E♭ Sonata (except its
Minuet and Trio) at the start of the Wielhorsky sketchbook. Since few
sketches have survived for the D minor Sonata and the finale of the G
major Sonata, and parts of the third and first movements of the E♭
Sonata, it is possible that Beethoven used loose leaves (which have sub-
sequently been lost) for preparatory work on these movements.

Among many critical issues arising from the sketches for the first
movement of Op. 31 no. 1, the evolution of the second subject is particularly intriguing. In the final version of the exposition, the second group
begins with a contredanse theme in B major, forming a striking tonal
contrast with the first subject's G major. This is followed by a tonally
unstable development of the theme in B minor, and the end of the
exposition is characterised by constant shifts between the major and
minor modes. But in the Kessler sketches for the second group, the contredanse theme appears consistently in B *minor*, a key whose tonic triad is
closer to G major. Example 3.4 shows an early concept sketch for the
contredanse theme and the closing idea of the exposition. In Beethoven's
first continuity sketch for the exposition, the closed eight-bar version of
the theme was replaced by a more complex reworking of the same ideas
(Example 3.5). B major makes a fleeting appearance here, giving a
momentary colour contrast at stave 9 bars 1 and 2: a feature that was not
retained in the next sketch for the passage. It was not until a second

Example 3.4 Kessler Sketchbook f. 91v staves 3 and 4

Example 3.5 Kessler Sketchbook f. 92r staves 7–11

continuity draft of the exposition on f. 93v of Kessler that Beethoven combined both the closed and reworked versions of the second subject from previous sketches into the composite form that appears in the final version. Yet even at this stage of the compositional process, B major played no part in the second group.

Example 3.6 Kessler Sketchbook f. 94v staves 8–10

Sketches for the first-movement coda of the G major Sonata cast unusual light on Nägeli's unauthorised reworking of the passage after the fermata in bar 295. The publisher's additions suggest that he disliked the isolation of the gesture in bars 296–8: it, alone, is unpaired with a balancing gesture in Beethoven's finished score, so Nägeli mistakenly added a tonic answer. But in Beethoven's continuity sketch for the recapitulation and coda, the rhythm ♪ ⁊♪⁊ | ♩ does indeed appear as part of a balanced series of repetitions, growing out of a large I–II⁷–V⁷ progression (Example 3.6). In the final version of the coda, the repetitions in Example 3.6 were replaced by a reprise of the first subject and brilliant-style passage work.

In the middle of an exposition draft for the first movement on f. 92v, Beethoven set down a concept sketch for the second movement, suggesting that he had clear ideas about the overall shape of the Adagio grazioso before he began any detailed work on paper (Example 3.7). In the course of thirteen bars the main theme, the C minor episode, and especially the coda are all captured in essence. Subsequent sketches for the Adagio explore different forms of melodic ornamentation, the tonal form of the C minor episode, and the form of the coda. A sketch for the coda on f. 96v suggests that at one stage Beethoven considered incorporating a cadenza-like passage (Example 3.8). The first eight bars have all the hallmarks of cadenza preparation, culminating in an implied second-inversion chord with a fermata. The next passage has several elements that are typical of classical cadenzas: it develops the opening theme very freely in imitative counterpoint; motivic working gives way to athematic

30

Example 3.7 Kessler Sketchbook f. 92v staves 1–6

Example 3.8 Kessler Sketchbook f. 96v staves 7-10

arpeggios; the 'cadenza' is extended by a move to the minor mode; and it ends with a trilled *Eingang* into the main theme. Although the generic background of the aria would have made this perfectly appropriate, perhaps Beethoven ultimately decided not to include this 'cadenza' in the movement's final version because he was already thinking forward to the coda of the finale, where just such a passage occurs.

Work on the finale of Op. 31 no. 1 and on the other two Op. 31 sonatas hardly extends beyond the stage of concept sketches in the Kessler sketchbook. And, as Barry Cooper has shown, the distance between the surviving sketches for the D minor Sonata and the finished work is very great.[36] The next group of substantial sketches comprises work on three movements of the E♭ Sonata on pages 1 to 11 of the Wielhorsky sketchbook. Beethoven must have made some sketches for the sonata before he began using Wielhorsky: two brief concept sketches for the first movement can be found in Kessler, and they have a remote bearing on the finished work's materials.[37] But in Wielhorsky there are no concept sketches for the Allegro, and work on the movement begins with continuity sketches of the development section (p. 2), recapitulation (p. 3) and coda (p. 4). These are very close to the final version in terms of their harmonic structure and length, though there are many differences in detail. For example, in the first continuity sketch for the development on page 2, Beethoven used the theme from bar 25 onwards as the basis for the modulatory passages; this was superseded at the bottom of the page by a second continuity sketch whose materials are much closer to the finished version. A tendency for the codas to be compressed during the sketching process is noticeable in both the G major and E♭ Sonatas. On page 4 the continuity sketch for the coda is rather longer than the final version: between bars 245 and 246 Beethoven reprised an extended 10-bar version of bars 153–60. Presumably he felt they were redundant, since he later cut them. Similarly, a sketch for the finale's coda (p. 11) gives a longer version that Beethoven eventually trimmed. The perfect cadence that ends the sonata is interrupted in the sketch by a 34-bar passage that reprises the theme from bar 13 onwards, leading to a fermata on c♭[3] and a brilliant-style liquidation of the opening theme. Perhaps the composer felt that the longer version of the coda contained too many fermatas, and that the 'extra' fermata on C♭ drew attention away from the structurally more significant ones on G♭. However, he

Example 3.9 Wielhorsky Sketchbook (a). p. 1 stave 2; (b). p. 1 stave 5; (c). p. 1 staves 6–7; (d). p. 4 staves 9–10; (e). p. 5 stave 5; (f). p. 5 stave 12

might simply have felt that the longer version of the coda unbalanced the movement's proportions.

Beethoven seems to have had some difficulties in fixing the character of the E♭ Sonata's unorthodox second movement, and he notated an unusually large number of concept sketches and variants for the opening theme. Six of these are listed in Example 3.9. Versions (a) to (c) are adjacent sketches on the first page of Wielhorsky. The first two appear without a clef, a tempo marking, or key and time signatures: both consist of two complementary four-bar phrases, with a head-motive outlining the pitch pattern C–D♭–E♭–F–D♭–C–B♭, but their elaboration suggests markedly different characters. The third version is marked 'al[legre]tto scherzo', and gives the first indication of the theme's extended binary form in the sonata. Yet the figuration in bars 3 and 4 was still provisional: these bars were fixed in the fourth version (sketched on page 4 of Wielhorsky), but now Beethoven had second thoughts about the shape of bars 1 and 2. A fifth (and ultimately the final) version, complete with offbeat *sforzati*, stands at the head of a continuity sketch of the exposition on page 5. Beethoven, though, still seems to have harboured doubts about the suitability of such a tuneful head-motive. At the foot of the same page he immediately began a second continuity sketch of the exposition, preserving the general outline of the opening theme, but transforming it into a (relatively characterless) *moto perpetuo*. Presumably he abandoned this version because of its banality and lack of rhythmic variety. In the continuity sketch for the development on page 7 he returned to version (e). No sketches for the recapitulation survive, though there are several concept sketches for the coda.

Editions

Although Beethoven contemplated a complete edition of his works, nothing came to fruition before his death.[38] But the Op. 27 and Op. 31 sonatas did appear in a number of editions during his lifetime. Simrock issued Op. 27 shortly after the appearance of Cappi's first edition in 1802. Subsequent German editions were published by Breitkopf and Härtel (1809), André (1810), and Schott (n.d.). In Paris, Pleyel brought out an edition of the C♯ minor Sonata in 1823 and the E♭ Sonata in the following year, and the London firm of Monzani and Hill issued both sonatas around 1823. In addition to the Nägeli and Simrock editions of Op. 31 nos. 1 and 2, Cappi issued a set of them in Vienna in 1803. The relationship between the three editions is not straightforward: in all probability the list of 'some 80 mistakes' in the Nägeli edition, which Beethoven sent to Simrock, was also acquired by Cappi, since many of the most obvious errors in Nägeli are corrected in the same way in the two subsequent editions.[39] But it is not clear to what extent all the differences between the editions are the result of Beethoven's proof-reading of Nägeli's defective copy, or are due to the composer taking the opportunity to refine details before the preparation of the new editions, or are indeed a matter of Simrock and Cappi introducing further misreadings into their texts. Both Simrock and (especially) Cappi copied some of Nägeli's mistakes, and Cappi introduced many more errors. One of Cappi's most serious misreadings was perpetuated in a large number of later nineteenth-century editions: the substitution of a left-hand chord f/A/D for Nägeli and Simrock's d/A/D at bar 226 in the first movement of the D minor Sonata. The early publishing history of the third sonata is more complex still: four separate editions appeared in 1804, the earliest (registered at Stationer's Hall on 3 September) by the London firm Clementi, Banger, Hyde, Collard and Davis.[40] Nägeli's edition probably appeared around the beginning of November, and those by Simrock and Cappi at about the same time.[41] Despite the London edition's chronological precedence its problematic relationship to the other early editions places a large question mark over its utility as a primary source for the sonata.[42] During Beethoven's lifetime all three Op. 31 sonatas appeared in editions by Hummel (1805), Kühnel (1806), André (1809), Schott (1821), and Böhme (1823).

The editors of these early editions (and for most of those that appeared in the twenty years after Beethoven's death) are anonymous, and the editing is minimal by modern scholarly standards. Since the composer played no part in their preparation, their textual variants must be viewed as a corruption of the more authentic earliest sources. Exceptionally, though, two editors who had close personal connections with Beethoven were named in early nineteenth-century editions: Carl Czerny (1791–1858) and Ignaz Moscheles (1794–1870). Czerny prepared texts of the sonatas for Haslinger's projected *Sämmtliche Werke von Ludw. van Beethoven* in 1828, and for Simrock's edition of the sonatas that appeared between 1856 and 1868. Moscheles edited the works for Cramer between around 1833 and 1839, and for Hallberger of Stuttgart in 1858. Since both men knew Beethoven's playing well, and Czerny had studied some of the sonatas with the composer, their metronome marks are of particular interest. But, as Sandra Rosenblum has shown, Czerny's concept of some movements changed quite radically between the late 1820s and the mid 1850s, with a general tendency towards slower tempi later in the century.[43] And Moscheles's editing, though described by one scholar as 'by the standards of his time accurate',[44] was nevertheless lax enough to include Nägeli's added bars in the first movement of Op. 31 no. 1 in the Hallberger edition.

New editions of Beethoven's sonatas saw their heyday between 1850 and 1880, when as many as forty-four complete editions were inaugurated.[45] Most were characterised by a pedagogical orientation and were edited by performers, many of them pupils of Czerny or Liszt, who added their own interpretative layer to texts which were already corrupt. Consequently their importance lies in what they reveal about nineteenth-century performance practices rather than as sources for reliable texts of the sonatas. In general, editorial accretions (which were rarely marked as such in the texts) consisted of adding metronome marks, pedalling, and dynamics; modifying articulation (especially by extending pre-existing slurs and adding more of them); and making changes to the voicing, stemming, and – occasionally – register of pitches. Where Beethoven had seemingly modified his ideas to contain them within the scope of his five-octave piano in the sonatas up to and including Op. 31, editors frequently extended the treble and bass lines to take advantage of modern 'improvements', as for example, in the treble at bar 54 in the second movement of Op. 31 no. 3, and the bass at bars 139–40 in the second movement of Op. 27 no. 1. Some editors went further still, doubling bass lines at the octave and thickening chords to produce richer sonorities suitable for performance in large public spaces. The attitude of many performer-editors was perhaps best summed up by one of its last and most fastidious practitioners. In the preface to his edition of the sonatas, Artur Schnabel wrote that 'the legato slurs as well as the accents and indications relative to touch were occasionally marked by the composer with such obvious, such confusing carelessness and negligence – particularly in the early works – that the editor felt himself not only musically justified, but in duty bound to change them now and then according to his best judgement, sense and taste: to abbreviate, to lengthen, to supplement, to interpret'.[46] Three editions of this type are of special interest because their editors were such distinguished performers of Beethoven's music. In Liszt's edition (Holle, Wolfenbüttel, 1857) the texts of the Op. 27 and Op. 31 sonatas contain relatively restrained editorial 'revisions', reflecting his mature view that

Beethoven's music should be performed unadorned (in contrast to his youthful practice: see pp. 48–9 below). As William Newman has remarked, the more colourful and individual aspects of Liszt's Beethoven interpretations are transmitted better by Hans von Bülow's contributions to the Cotta edition of the sonatas (Stuttgart, 1871), including both Op. 27 sonatas and Op. 31 no. 3.[47] The most detailed performance indications appear in Schnabel's edition (Ullstein, Berlin, 1924–7). He discusses nuances of articulation and voicing in minute detail: for instance, he supplements Beethoven's unprecedentedly detailed marking at the head of the C♯ minor sonata with 'dolcissimo, cantando, con intimissiom sentimento ma molto semplice, non patetico e sempre bene in tempo e misura' at the upbeat to bar 6. In addition to the metronome markings at the start of each movement, he also gives figures for more subtle shifts of tempo within movements; there are, for example, five such changes in the last 13 bars of Op. 27 no. 2, ranging from ♩ = 66 (bars 188–9) to ♩ = 108 (bars 196–8).

In contrast to the mixture of practical advice and poetic interpretations of the music's character which 'performing' editions offered amateur players, other editions presented the sonatas within a theoretical framework, designed to give performers analytical insights. One of the most widely used was Hugo Riemann's edition (Simrock, Berlin, 1889) which gives detailed analyses of phrasing, and indicates important formal subdivisions within movements. Riemann's influence is apparent in George Sporck's edition of the sonatas (Paris, 1907–13) with its analytical rephrasing of Beethoven's texts. Sporck ignored most of Beethoven's dynamics, and wrote his own detailed set designed to underpin his conception of the phrasing. Marginal notes highlight important points in the formal articulation of each movement, and draw attention to 'hidden' motivic relationships. Stuart McPherson's 'analytical edition' of the sonatas (Williams, London, 1909–23) was less ambitious in scope, merely prefacing each sonata with a short and simple set of formal analyses. McPherson's musical texts are typical pedagogical products, with thick layers of editorial accretions. Other editions were intended to be used in conjunction with book-length studies of the sonatas: Fritz Vollbach's edition (Tanger, Cologne, 1919) has annotations that are explicated in his *Erläuterungen zu dem Klaviersonaten Beethovens* (1919); and Tovey's much-used *Companion to*

Beethoven's Pianoforte Sonatas (1935) was written in conjunction with Harold Craxton's edition of the sonatas (Associated Board, London, 1931), for which Tovey had already provided pedagogical prefaces.

If the increasing professionalisation of musicology may be perceived in the theoretical emphasis of the editions mentioned above, then it had more profound consequences on changing attitudes towards what constituted a good text in the first place. Few nineteenth-century editors were concerned with producing a text that 'objectively' reflected the original sources, though Theodore Steingräber did make an effort to consult some manuscripts and early editions for his complete edition of the sonatas (Mittler, Leipzig, 1874).[48] Breitkopf and Härtel's 1862–3 edition (still available in Lea Pocket Scores and in other formats) was also advertised as being 'corrected with reference to the original editions', but no editor was named, no critical notes included, and none of the sources was identified in detail. Moreover, the text is deeply flawed by modern scholarly standards: the reading of the Op. 31 sonatas, for example, incorporates numerous errors from corrupt early sources. But in the early decades of the twentieth century, a number of editors took greater pains to remove the editorial accretions that had long disfigured the sonatas. Heinrich Schenker's edition (Universal, Vienna, 1901–18) was the first to be based on a systematic study of available autographs and first and early editions, though Schenker added copious fingering suggestions.[49] Even some 'performing' editions from the 1920s (most notably Schnabel's) made careful distinctions between editorial performance indications and phrasing, articulation, and pedalling from early sources. The most thorough attempt to present a 'clean' text based entirely on the earliest authentic sources was Bertha Wallner's edition for Henlé (Duisburg, 1952–3), and this, together with a re-evaluation of the primary sources, formed the basis of Hans Schmidt's edition in the new *Beethoven Werke* (Duisburg, 1970s).[50] A detailed commentary on Schmidt's edition of the Op. 27 and Op. 31 sonatas has yet to appear, and, given the complexity of the sources for Op. 31, this is a major drawback in the usefulness of the edition. Though Schmidt's texts can be recommended to performers they are not flawless. Beethoven's varied articulation marks (from delicate dots to vigorous slashes) are homogenised as dots by Schmidt, even though the earliest editions of the sonatas preserve the fundamental distinction, albeit inconsistently. And in the Op.

31 sonatas, Schmidt's slurring occasionally conflates readings from the three primary sources. Of course, the concept of *an* Urtext for the Op. 31 sonatas is a chimera. With the recent publication of facsimiles of the Nägeli and Simrock editions (though not, unfortunately, of the Cappi and London editions), performers are now better placed to make their own choices between the variants.

While scholarly editions have attempted to be ever more faithful to Beethoven's conception, a large number of populist publications have moved in precisely the opposite direction. The numerous transcriptions of movements from the Op. 27 and Op. 31 sonatas alone would make a fascinating study of popular Beethoven reception. During the composer's lifetime Op. 31 no. 1 appeared in transcriptions for string quartet (Simrock, 1807–8) and string trio (André, 1818). Simrock also published string quartet arrangements of the first and last movements of Op. 27 no. 1 and the middle movement of Op. 27 no. 2 in 1822. But the vogue for taking movements out of context and transcribing them for different forces really took off later in the nineteenth century. Naturally, the opening Adagio sostenuto of the C♯ minor Sonata received this treatment far more often than any other movement. It was often transcribed for voices, with penitential liturgical or religious texts (as in G. B. ' Bierey's Kyrie for choir and orchestra published by Breitkopf and Härtel in 1831), or as morose songs (such as Schiller's *Resignation*, arranged by Wilhelmine von Bock), and the combinations of instruments for which it has been transcribed include organ, piano and violin (Nicou-Choron), military band (E. Dovin), guitar (Arturo Langerotti), and even the zither (J. Grienauer). These are not so much editions of the sonata as independent works. On a higher artistic plane, the Trio of Op. 31 no. 3 formed the basis for a set of variations for two pianos by Saint-Saëns (Op. 35, 1874).

Critics

Given the essentially private environment in which piano sonatas were played in most parts of Europe at the beginning of the nineteenth century, it is not surprising that there are very few reports of performances in the years immediately after the publication of Op. 27 and Op. 31. Nevertheless, if – as Czerny reported – Beethoven once exclaimed that 'Everyone always talks about the C♯ minor Sonata!', then that work, at least, must have caused something of a sensation.[51] Critical responses – in the press, journals, pedagogical books, and monographs – are largely the work of those who engaged with music professionally. Though they reflect the views of performers and thinkers who may have influenced amateur opinion, they reveal little directly about the reception of the sonatas in the widespread sphere of amateur music-making.

In the early reception history of the sonatas, critics engaged primarily with the music's poetic content, highlighting the subjectivity of their responses by constructing imaginative extra-musical metaphors to communicate their critical insights. The sonatas appeared during a transitional phase in the press reception of Beethoven's music. By 1802 reviews of his latest works in the influential Leipzig *Allgemeine musikalische Zeitung* had become more sympathetic to the values of difficulty and complexity enshrined in his music, but they did not yet attempt the type of detailed exegesis pioneered by E. T. A. Hoffmann's reading of the Fifth Symphony in 1810. When a critic reviewed the Op. 27 sonatas (along with Op. 26) in the *AMZ* on 30 June 1802, he took for granted the high quality of the music. Emphasising the elitism of the sonatas, he warned off unsuspecting amateurs, and set out to disparage the taste of those who might object to music of such technical and intellectual complexity. He believed that the difficulties were justified because they were a *necessary* vehicle for the profound sentiments Beethoven wanted to express in his music: the composer had a supreme understanding of the instrument; the figures were not 'without effect', and they served the music's principal quality, 'expression'; the 'horrible key' of C♯ minor was used 'for good reasons'. The composer no longer had a duty to avoid giving his public these difficulties. Rather, the burden of debt had been reversed so that the public was now beholden to the composer: only the best instruments and diligent, studious performers would do justice to the music.

These are the three compositions for pianoforte with which Herr v. B. has recently enriched the choice collections of educated musicians and skilled pianists. Enriched – for they are a true enrichment and belong (especially [Op.27 no. 2]) to the few of this year's products that will last. The editor need not repeat the praise given to new Beethoven works by others elsewhere in these pages. Such praise may be applied completely to the present pieces, and is well known to the type of music-lover for whom Beethoven writes, and who is in the position to follow and relish [his music]. To those who are less educated or who want their music to be no more than a light amusement, these works would be recommended in vain. It only remains for the editor to make a few brief remarks here. In places [Op. 26] is worked out with excessive artifice. But in no way could this be said about the truly great, sombre, and magnificent movement that, in order to point the player in the right direction, the editor inscribes 'Marcia funebre sulla morte d'un Eroe', since here all that is difficult and elaborate serves the principal aspect [of the music]: expression. Those who complain of the difficulty of the ideas or their execution in this movement (as in various places in [Op. 27 no. 1] and almost the whole of [Op. 27 no. 2]) resemble popular philosophers who like to conduct each profound discourse in the language of a polite tea-time conversation. In [Op. 27 no. 1] the editor found the first three movements (up to page 5) to be quite excellent; but the short final Presto – which had the same effect as the typical noisy ending in large, elaborate Italian opera arias – did not strike him as good. However, [Op. 27 no. 2] is beyond reproach. This fantasy is from beginning to end a sterling whole, at once sprung from the whole of a deep and ardent imagination, and at the same time hewn from a block of marble. It is quite impossible that anyone on whom nature has bestowed musicality should not be affected and gradually transported ever higher by the first Adagio (which the publisher has quite rightly inscribed: *Si deve suonare tutto questo pezzo delicatissimamente e senza sordino*), and then be moved so ardently and transported by the Presto agitato, as only freely-conceived piano music can transport him. These two principal movements are written in the horrible key of C sharp minor for good reasons; ... On the evidence of the markings, and even more obviously, the whole plan and the disposition of his ideas, B[eethoven] understands how to handle the properties and excellences of the pianoforte like hardly any other composer for this instrument, just as C. P. E. Bach understood how to handle the real clavier [i.e. the clavichord]. One must possess an extremely good instrument if one wants to do justice to the performance of many of his movements – e.g. the whole first movement of [Op. 27 no. 2]. Since the editor would not complain about performance difficulties if they were necessary for the representation of a significant idea, he has already mentioned – and one must give Herr v[an] B[eethoven] his due – that in his compositions of this type the figures that are hard to perform are not, as they sometimes are in Clementi, without effect. But Hr. v[an] B[eethoven] should not burden enthusiasts of his compositions with movements that can be played properly only by those with extraordinarily large hands. The composer who knows how to repay them can rightly demand study, diligence, and effort; . . . [52]

What the critic seems to have especially admired about the C♯ minor Sonata, then, was the way in which Beethoven had given free rein to his fantasy ('sprung from . . . [an] ardent imagination') while maintaining the most solid coherence ('hewn from a block of marble'). But while all the sonatas are praised, there is an obvious imbalance in the treatment of the two Op. 27 sonatas. In the context of a review that values the high originality of the music, his comment that the E♭ Sonata closes like 'a *typical* noisy ending' of an aria seems damning; while, on the other hand, the C♯ minor Sonata is 'beyond reproach'.

On their publication in 1803 the first two Op. 31 sonatas were ignored by the *AMZ*, but Nägeli's edition was reviewed by J. G. K. Spazier in the Leipzig-based *Zeitung für die elegante Welt*. Spazier echoed Nägeli's advertisements for the *Répertoire des Clavecinistes*, remarking on the grand style of the music, and the fact that the works deviated from the usual form of the sonata. But he was not wholly positive about this, finding a certain 'casualness' in the connections between different parts of the sonatas; the perceived lack of coherence was compounded by the fact that the sonatas were both 'a little too long' and 'bizarre in places'.[53] In contrast to almost all subsequent critics, he found the G major Sonata the more original of the two. Four years later, the same journal carried a more favourable review of the E♭ Sonata, which the reviewer considered to be 'one of the most original and beautiful works of the brilliant Beethoven'.[54] The richness and variety of Beethoven's music was no longer perceived as detrimental to its effectiveness. Rather, 'its affective expression is nuanced in so many different ways, now tender, gentle, and intimate, now speaking to the heart with heroic power, that the unity of the whole, with all its contrasts, enchants and thrills'. In the same way that the *AMZ* critic had attempted to justify the demands made on amateur pianists by the Op. 27 sonatas, the reviewer advised that 'this sonata, like most of Beethoven's, must be played many times for all its subtleties and its grand character to be understood and performed properly; moreover it demands a proficient eye and dexterous hand from performers'.

In contrast to these two early reviews of the Op. 31 sonatas, almost all subsequent critics have lavished most attention on the D minor Sonata. Similarly, the greater detail in which the C♯ minor Sonata was treated by the *AMZ* critic, and the more effusive response it solicited, set the pattern for the subsequent critical reception of the Op. 27 sonatas. Why should this have been so? Does it merely reflect remarkably consistent aesthetic judgements on these particular sonatas? Or might it be symptomatic of deeper cultural values? Robert Hatten has attributed these sonatas' critical ascendancy to the semiotic markedness of the minor mode: 'if minor correlates with a narrower range of meaning than major, then works in minor should tend to provoke more-specific expressive interpretations than works in major . . . Indeed, if one considers some of the early- and middle-period Beethoven piano sonatas, one finds that the minor mode movements . . . are the focus of much greater critical attention, and more specific expressive interpretation, than the major mode movements.'[55]

This is certainly true of the poetic responses that the two minor-mode sonatas drew from critics in the early nineteenth century. Czerny, discussing the character of each of Beethoven's piano sonatas, was more effusive in his description of Op. 27 no. 2 and Op. 31 no. 2 than with the other sonatas in each set.[56] For him, the opening of the C♯ minor Sonata was 'a nocturnal scene, in which a mournful ghostly voice sounds from the distance' and the D minor Sonata possessed 'a remarkably sustained tragic character' and was full of 'Romantic-picturesque' elements. In contrast, his comments on the other sonatas were more prosaic: the E♭ Sonata from Op. 27 was described as 'more of a fantasia than its companion' due to the type and distribution of its movements;[57] the middle movement of Op. 31 no. 1 was likened to a 'graceful Romanze or a Notturno', in which, during the final reprise of the main theme, the bass should imitate a guitar accompaniment; Op. 31 no. 3 was seen to be 'more rhetorical than pictorial' in character, its 'spirited joviality' in complete contrast to the 'elegiac-romantic' character of the preceding sonata. Similarly, Berlioz reserved some of his most imaginative critical metaphors for the C♯ minor Sonata. Responding to a performance by Liszt in April 1835, he wrote that the first movement 'is the sun setting over the Roman countryside. All is profoundly sad, calm, majestic, and solemn. The fiery globe descends slowly behind the cross of St Peter, which is detached, glittering, from the horizon: no living being disturbs the peace of the tombs that cover this desolate earth, one contemplates . . . one admires . . . one weeps . . . one is silent.'[58]

Against the background of a critical culture that revelled in such poetic responses, it seems inevitable that the two minor-mode sonatas should have acquired sobriquets during the first half of the nineteenth century. According to Lenz, Op. 27 no. 2 became known as the 'Moonlight' Sonata around 1830 when connoisseurs in Germany took up Ludwig Rellstab's image of the Adagio sostenuto: 'a boat visiting the wild places on Lake Lucerne by moonlight'.[59] It is tempting to believe that some of Beethoven's contemporaries were familiar with this imagery. In 1826, Schubert's 1815 setting of Hölty's *An den Mond* ('To the Moon') was published with an inauthentic three-bar piano introduction which exhibits such strong similarities with the opening of Beethoven's sonata that it is difficult not to hear it as a parody.[60] If Op. 27 no. 2 has an inauthentic sobriquet, then that of Op. 31 no. 2 has some claims to authenticity. Anton Schindler reported that he once asked Beethoven to elucidate the meaning of the sonatas Op. 31 no. 2 and Op. 57. The composer's terse reply – 'Just read Shakespeare's *Tempest*' – has both intrigued and frustrated critics ever since it came to light in the 1840s.[61] Since the publisher Cranz had earlier (1838) dubbed Op. 57 'Appassionata', the name 'The Tempest' has been solely applied to Op. 31 no. 2.

Some later critics have taken these sobriquets as cues for elaborate extra-musical programmes, but most twentieth-century reaction to them has ranged from amused tolerance to hostile rejection. Hostility has arisen from two directions: formalist critics have argued that, since the names are extraneous, they cannot have any bearing on the inner workings of the music and are therefore irrelevant; those who are more predisposed to acknowledging a poetic dimension in music criticism have mistrusted their usefulness, viewing them as either too general, or as only selectively appropriate. Yet the names persist. And it could be argued that they are important, not as keys to interpreting the sonatas, but in what they reveal about the works' reception. 'Moonlight' stands as an apt symbol for the Romantic tendency to evoke the sublime in relation to Beethoven's instrumental music. Czerny too conjured up a nocturnal scene in relation to this particular movement, and Berlioz the awe-struck contemplation of a classical twilight. Though the fact that it has been such a durable tag for the C♯ minor Sonata may be due in part to lazy habits, it also shows how much the popular imagination has divorced the opening Adagio sostenuto from its context within the sonata as a whole.[62] Parallels between the construction of Beethoven's posthumous reputation in Germany and that of Shakespeare provide a broader context for understanding the significance of 'The Tempest' and Op. 31 no. 2.[63] From the 1830s there was a marked tendency for German critics to compare Beethoven's genius with Shakespeare's. The most glaring example of the 'Shakespearianisation' of Beethoven is the misappropriation of *Coriolan* as a Shakespearian work (it was in fact written for a play by Heinrich von Collin). Beethoven himself seems to have initiated the critical trope. His repeated references to covert Shakespearian programmes in his works was grist to the mill of critics and biographers who wished to bolster his cultural authority by yoking it with the supreme figure in the European literary pantheon.[64] In this way, Schindler's anecdote might be seen as forming part of the power play of cultural politics in the 1840s, whatever its significance as a problematically nebulous reference to a possible covert programme.

If the dominant strand in nineteenth-century Beethoven criticism was founded on the belief that his music could best be elucidated by colourful poetic imagery, then an alternative view held that in order truly to understand the spirit animating Beethoven's music it is necessary to engage with its technical details. One of the pioneers in this field was A. B. Marx (1795–1866), Beethoven's most redoubtable critical champion in mid-nineteenth-century Germany. For Marx, Beethoven was the greatest composer of ideal music, and the composer's conception of sonata form was the paramount vehicle for the musical coherence demanded by ideal music.[65] In his hugely influential treatise on composition, which appeared during the 1840s, Marx's discussion of this ultimate classical form centred on a technical discussion of movements from Beethoven's sonatas, with particularly full treatment given to the first movements of Op. 31 nos. 1 and 3.[66] Such an approach only became widespread, however, in the early decades of the twentieth century, following a gradual critical trend in the late nineteenth century towards de-contextualising artworks and emphasising their structural autonomy. Several important theorists from this era analysed aspects of

Beethoven's sonatas, including Hugo Riemann (1849–1919) and – ultimately more influentially – Heinrich Schenker (1868–1935).[67] In the decades since World War II, when analysis has become a core musicological discipline, Beethoven's sonatas have offered a rich vein for analytical inquiry, leading to the appearance of numerous studies of the sonatas. Some of this work will be invoked in due course.

The professionalisation of musicology has inevitably affected other areas of Beethoven scholarship and criticism. Pioneering work on Beethoven's working processes by Gustav Nottebohm (1817–82) has been refined, and published transcriptions of the source sketchbooks for Opp. 27 and 31 have been made by Miculicz (1927), Fischman (1962) and Brandenburg (1976).[68] Renewed interest in performance on period instruments has in part been fuelled by research into the notational practices and performing styles of the late eighteenth and early nineteenth centuries, and this aspect of Beethoven's keyboard music has been subjected to detailed scrutiny in several studies, notably Newman (1972), Rosenblum (1988), Komlós (1995) and Barth (1995).[69] Naturally, what these studies have highlighted above all else is a gradual but profound shift in performing styles between Beethoven's day and ours, and this forms the topic of the following paragraphs.

Pianists

Though there are many contemporaneous accounts of Beethoven's improvisations, few reports give technical and interpretative details relating to his performances of his published works. Only one such anecdote refers to any of the sonatas from 1802–3. Ferdinand Ries recalled that Beethoven chose to play his newly published D minor Sonata at a salon in 1803. Earlier that evening Ries had been publicly ticked off by the composer for some inaccuracies in his playing. When Beethoven himself came to play, a princess 'who probably expected that [he] too would make a mistake somewhere' stood behind him. All went well until bars 53 and 54 in the first movement, where 'Beethoven missed the entry, and instead of descending two notes and then two more, he struck each crotchet in the descending passage with his whole hand (three or four notes at once). It sounded as if the piano was being cleaned. The Princess rapped him several times around the head, not at all delicately, saying: "If the pupil receives one tap of the finger for one missed note, then the master must be punished with a full hand for worse mistakes." Everyone laughed, Beethoven most of all. He started again and performed marvellously. The Adagio in particular was incomparably played.'[70]

The most comprehensive early-nineteenth-century source of information about performing Beethoven's sonatas is Czerny's essay *Über den richtigen Vortrag der sämtlichen Beethoven'schen Sonaten für das Piano allein* (1842). As a pupil of the composer, Czerny had been in the rare position of being able to observe Beethoven's performances of his own works and to take his advice on matters of performance. He studied the D minor Sonata with the composer, and it has been suggested (from the evidence of the essay) that he must also have worked on the C♯ minor Sonata with him. Moreover, other pianists who knew Beethoven's playing commented on the reliability of Czerny's advice regarding suitable tempi for Beethoven's music.[71] Thus Czerny's comments are of special interest in that they appear to represent the nearest thing we have to an authentic source of detailed information on performing the sonatas.

In the opening section of his essay Czerny emphasises the need for players to be faithful to Beethoven's text: no additions or abbreviations are tolerable.[72] He stresses the importance of choosing suitable tempi and gives another set of metronome marks (which differ from his Haslinger and Simrock sets). Most importantly, from the perspective of performance history, he reads beyond the letter of Beethoven's scores to discuss un-notated technical issues like pedalling and fingering, and interpretative questions such as rubato and nuances of colour. The following paragraphs summarise his comments on the Op. 27 and Op. 31 sonatas.

Tempo variation: Czerny gives specific instances of passages which call for tempo variation and rubato. For example, in the first movement of the C♯ minor Sonata bars 32–5 should contain a crescendo to *forte* and an accelerando, and bars 36–9 a diminuendo and ritardando back to the original levels of dynamics and tempo. In the finale he suggests that a ritardando might be made in each of the following bars: 13, 50, 52, 55 and 56. In the middle movement of the D minor Sonata, he suggests making a crescendo to *forte* and accelerando for three bars beginning at bar 55, and a compensatory rallentando and diminuendo beginning at bar 58.

However, elsewhere he warns that a strict tempo should be maintained, as in the finale of Op. 27 no. 1, the first movement of Op. 31 no. 1, and the Scherzo of Op. 31 no. 3.

Pedalling: Czerny re-interprets and supplements Beethoven's meagre pedalling marks. He takes the famous 'senza sordino' instruction at the top of the C# minor Sonata to indicate that the pedal should be used constantly, but changed with each change of harmony. In the sonata's finale he recommends that it should be changed every half-bar in bars 55–6 (and at the parallel place in the recapitulation), and that in the movement's closing bars the dampers should be raised throughout. Detailed advice is similarly given about the D minor Sonata. In the first movement the pedal should be used through the *forte* bars from bar 21 onwards (and at parallel places in the development and recapitulation). During the 'recitative' passages (bars 143–8 and 153–8) the dampers should be lifted throughout, so that the single line should sound like 'a distant lament'. And in the last ten bars they should be raised throughout the long stretch of D minor harmony, so that the quaver figures in the bass sound 'like distant thunder'. Czerny also suggests that the pedal should be used liberally in the other two movements of Op. 31 no. 2, as long as care is taken to dampen changes of harmony.

If Czerny might be seen as the chief exponent of a performing tradition stemming in part from the composer's own style of playing, then an alternative virtuoso approach was most brilliantly represented by the early career of his most famous pupil, Franz Liszt. By all accounts, Liszt's performances of Beethoven's sonatas powerfully conveyed the character of the works, but he accomplished this by taking startling liberties with the texts, appropriating them to his own ends. Beethoven became in Liszt's hands a tragic-heroic figure whose music is above all about expressive intensity, elemental power, and the sublime. It is not perhaps surprising, then, that he played Op. 27 no. 2 and Op. 31 no. 2 in public more often than any other Beethoven sonatas, or that the witty, ironic, anarchic Op. 31 nos. 1 and 3, and the predominantly lyrical Op. 27 no. 1 were not in his public repertoire at all.[73] The types of liberties he took are captured in the many reports of his performances of the C# minor Sonata. When he played it at the Hôtel de Ville in Paris on 9 April 1835, the Adagio sostenuto was given in an orchestral arrangement by Narcisse Girard, and Liszt played only the last two movements.[74] Berlioz was sent into poetic raptures by the performance (see his response, above), but other critics were less impressed. In the *Revue Musicale* the critic liked the orchestral arrangement, and conceded that Liszt's genius was one of the most interesting and unusual of the age. But he felt that the violence of the performer's feelings had led him to commit musical errors, such as his constant variations of tempo in the Menuetto and the way in which he chopped up the phrases in the Finale.[75] Yet if Liszt was sometimes guilty of playing to the gallery in his youth, he could also take a more subtle approach when the occasion demanded. Thus Berlioz contrasted two other performances of the C♯ minor Sonata in the early 1830s. At the first of these, Liszt disfigured the Adagio sostenuto in a manner 'designed to win applause from the fashionable public': he added liberal accelerandi and ritardandi, trills, and tremolos, which Berlioz likened to the 'rumbling of thunder in a cloudless sky, where darkness is caused only by the setting of the sun'. A few years later Berlioz heard him play the same movement in darkness before a select gathering of people at the house of Ernest Legouvé. On this occasion 'the noble elegy . . . emerged in its sublime simplicity; not a single note, not a single accent was added to the composer's accents and notes. It was the ghost of Beethoven, evoked by the virtuoso, whose great voice we heard'.[76] According to Kastner, Liszt later regretted the liberties he had taken wih Beethoven's music during his youth, and after his regular recital tours ended he seems to have inclined towards greater textual fidelity.[77]

In the later nineteenth century many prominent pianists followed Liszt's example, programming Beethoven's sonatas selectively and reinterpreting the music from an elaborately virtuosic perspective. Aspects of Liszt's selectivity even trickled down to the large amateur sphere. For example, under the heading 'A Selection of Good Pianoforte Music', Carl Engel's *The Pianist's Hand-book* (London, 1853) recommended the C♯ minor and D minor Sonatas, but not the others from Op. 27 and Op. 31.[78] However, it would be mistaken to see Liszt as entirely representative of pianistic culture in the mid- nineteenth century. Public performances of Beethoven's sonatas were still rare in many parts of Europe, and the tragic-heroic sonatas did not enjoy a complete stranglehold on the repertoire. Charles Hallé told how one London impresario was astonished by his request to play a Beethoven sonata in public in 1848, and even more surprised that he had chosen the E♭ Sonata from

Op. 31; but it pleased so much that 'several ladies who heard it arranged afternoon parties to hear it once more'.[79] As Beethoven's position as a culturally dominant personality became ever stronger, so public exposure to a larger number of the sonatas became more common. Hallé was one of the first pianists to play a complete cycle of the sonatas in public (1861). But for many, the pianist of the post-Liszt generation who was most synonymous with Beethoven's music was Liszt's pupil and son-in-law, Hans von Bülow. Contemporary reports suggest that Bülow's interpretation of Beethoven was less flamboyant than Liszt's early manner. Henry Krebheil described it as appealing to 'those who wish to add intellectual enjoyment to the pleasures of the imagination', though Clara Schumann was reported to find it 'calculated', and James Huneker thought it 'pedantic'.[80] Yet if Bülow's editions of the sonatas give some indication of his performances, then he must have played with more freedom of tempo and dynamic re-interpretation than is common in many recorded peformances from the modern era.

Despite the tangential evidence contained in performer's editions, eye-witness reports and critiques, much of the detail of individual nineteenth-century performances remains frustratingly elusive. In the age of recordings, though, the abundance of material gives a much fuller picture, but its sheer volume produces methodological difficulties for a survey such as this. The following paragraphs discuss recordings of the C♯ minor Sonata by a small number of pianists who have become renowned for their playing of Beethoven.[81] This is intended to sketch some of the more prominent trends in performing styles in the last seventy-five years, and should not be taken as comprehensive.

Before discussing the differences of approach that distinguish one generation of pianists from another, it should be stressed that some aspects of the sonata are interpreted with a remarkable unanimity across the generation gaps. All but one of the pianists surveyed here take on board Czerny's advice about tempo fluctuation in the first movement, though the degree of fluctuation varies considerably. Hardly any pianist plays accurately the characteristic dotted anacrusis in the melody of the Adagio sostenuto, the exceptions being Solomon (whose accuracy can sound pedantic), and Gilels (who avoids this pitfall by taking a faster tempo and using more rubato). Friedman and Backhaus shorten the semiquaver so much that the motive sounds almost double dotted in their hands, and others – though less extreme —shorten the semiquaver to a sextuplet, with half the length of the underlying triplets. Most of the players establish a strict tempo relationship between the central Allegretto and one or other of the movements on either side of it. Most commonly, this affects of the Adagio sostenuto: Friedman sets a tempo of ♩ = ♩. = 46, Lamond 72–6, Schnabel 63, Backhaus 58–60, and Immerseel 54–8. Solomon, Bilson and Lubin link the second and third movements in this way, all setting an underlying tempo of ♩. = ♩ = 84. Serkin, Gilels and Brendel do not establish such tempo relationships. The most pervasive agreement in all these performances concerns the basic pulse of the finale at ♩ = *c.* 84. In general, short-term tempo fluctuations are also most common in this movement: all players observe a slower tempo at the start of the second subject, followed by an accelerando back to ♩ = *c.* 84 in bars 21–29; and many allow the tempo to push forward slightly during climactic semiquaver passagework. But again, the degree of rubato varies considerably from performance to performance.

Some of the earliest recordings of Beethoven's sonatas were made by pupils of Liszt and Bülow (such as Frederick Lamond, 1868–1948), and of Czerny's pupil Theodore Lechetizsky (for example, Ignaz Friedman, 1882–1948, and Artur Schnabel, 1882–1951). Their performances are distinguished by fluidity of tempo, strong characterisation of expressive details, and – in some cases – a cavalier attitude towards Beethoven's markings. Whether or not these qualities reflect in detail the performance styles of the pianists' distinguished nineteenth-century teachers, their spontaneity certainly emphasises the fantasy elements in the C♯ minor Sonata. However, such characteristics occasionally become obtrusive in Friedman's recording from the 1920s. He alters Beethoven's text in several places, ignoring the repeat signs in the middle movement, playing the Trio (♩ = 132) at a slower tempo than the Allegretto (144), and adding lower octaves to the bass at bars 102 and 190 in the finale. There is a leisurely attitude towards the Adagio sostenuto (♩ = *c.* 46), and Friedman uses rubato selectively with different voices, so that the melody is not always co-ordinated with its accompaniment, especially at bars 15–19 and 51–5. The Allegretto is one of the slowest on record, and its opposition of articulations (staccato and legato) is underlined by heavy tempo fluctuations. In contrast, Friedman's performance of the finale is very rapid and fiery. While the initial excitement of his tempo cannot be denied, it results in some loss of technical control later in the movement. The tempo slows suddenly at more lyrical passages, leading to a loss of momentum, so that the climactic return of the fantasy style in the coda loses much of its potential eloquence.

Frederick Lamond's reading integrates details more convincingly within the music's broad sweep. His Adagio sostenuto is brisk by the standards of the other recordings ($\downarrow = c.$ 76) but it has a fluency – a true *alla breve* gait – matched only by Schnabel and (to a lesser extent) Bilson. Lamond's accompanying triplets are more prominent than usual, enriching the texture and leading into the central triplet-dominated section without the sudden change of focus that mars some other interpretations. In the Allegretto Lamond, like Friedman, applies different degrees of rubato to separate voices, so that the melody sometimes arrives at a bar line after the accompanying chords. To today's ears the effect is initially unsettling, but it has an advantage over more modern 'co-ordinated' rubato in that it carries expressive weight without compromising the dance's rhythmic momentum. His Presto agitato is stormy, but its effects are achieved by careful articulation and voicing, rather than sheer speed. Lamond's rubato is more subtle than Friedman's, fixed within narrower limits, and seeming to emerge organically from the music's gestures and the ebb and flow of its harmonic tension. The performance thus accumulates a strong momentum, and, for visceral excitement, his playing of the coda is second to none. He whips forcefully through the diminished seventh chords in bars 163–6, and captures the coda's quicksilver changes from extroversion to introversion with a remarkable spontaneity; yet his finely judged increase in weight through the arpeggiated chords in bars 177–84 evinces a cool sense of the music's trajectory.

Artur Schnabel's justly famous 1934 recording has many of the same sterling qualities, though they are often achieved in different ways. His tempi are slower than Lamond's, and his rubato and tempo fluctuations are heavier, but he has the same convincing ability to give due emphasis to details without distorting the flow of the music. Even more than in Lamond's recording, Schnabel's rubato in the first movement seems to grow out of an acute sensitivity to the tensions and relaxations within each phrase. Additionally, Schnabel projects melodic lines with a greater finesse, using a wider range of tone to create more subtle and varied expressive nuances. In comparison, the performance by Solomon (1902–88) sounds both wilful and unidiomatic. He plays the first two movements 'straight' with an unparalled rigidity of tempo and phrasing, and he ignores Beethoven's *alla breve* time signature for the Adagio sostenuto, setting a tempo of ♩ = *c*. 32. But in the finale a very heavy rubato is used, and the tempo fluctuates between ♩ = 100 (the first subject's semiquaver arpeggios) and 66 (the start of the second subject).

In recordings from the 1950s and 60s a new trend emerges. A sense of spontaneity is less evident, and complete technical control is never sacrificed to expressive immediacy. The intensity of many performances seems to stem instead from the accumulation of momentum, in readings which tend to subsume the expressive potential of individual details to the long-term unfolding of musical form. A monumental approach to the Adagio sostenuto is noticeable in several performances, whether they take a measured tone (like Rudolf Serkin's 1963 reading at ♩ = 44) or a cooler, faster approach (such as Wilhelm Backhaus at ♩ = *c*. 58 in 1958). None of the recordings from this period are marked by the type of overt idiosyncrasies that feature in some from the pre-war era, such as Solomon's extremes of tempo, or Friedman's heavy rubato and registral amplifications. But the warmth of recorded performances such as those of Emil Gilels (early 1980s) and Alfred Brendel (1970) retain the individuality of the best early recordings while subscribing to more modern values. Whether prompted by improving recording techniques or purely from an evolving aesthetic, many post-war recordings are characterised by greater textural clarity: pianists use the sustaining pedal more sparingly and discreetly, and passagework in the Presto agitato is usually captured in almost clinical detail. The pianists who capitalise on this most successfully are Serkin and Brendel: their technical virtuosity in itself raises the expressive temperature of the performances, and is yoked to the music's tonal and thematic dramas to thrilling effect.

Finally, the most modern trend in performances has been a return to the instruments of Beethoven's era and the exploration of their possibilities in the light of recent scholarship on contemporaneous performance practices. In general, these performances have highlighted the extent to which Beethoven's music stretched the capabilities of the instruments available to him: the stormiest passages can be played with a ferocity that might sound overblown on a modern instrument. But the most obvious pay-offs have been in those movements that pose the most severe technical problems for players on modern instruments, notably the pedalling and delicacy called for in the Adagio sostenuto of the C$\sharp$ minor Sonata, and in the 'recitative' passages from the first movement of the D minor Sonata. In his 1997 performance of Op. 27 no. 2 on a modern copy of a five-octave Schantz piano of *c.* 1800, Malcolm Bilson takes Beethoven's marking '*sempre pianissimo e senza sordino*' literally, playing the entire Adagio sostenuto with the dampers raised and the moderator engaged. At a tempo of ♪ = *c.* 56 and with the dynamic level kept to a bare minimum the resonance of the instrument creates a thin haze of sound around the notated pitches without creating obtrusive dissonances, except in the faster-moving bass at bars 48–9 and 56–8. Unlike many performers on modern instruments, Bilson plays all three movements without a break, imitating the continuity Beethoven called for in the first of the fantasy sonatas, and underlines the continuity by establishing a strict tempo relationship between the Allegretto (♩. = 84) and the Presto agitato (♩ = 84). In this respect he takes a similar approach to Steven Lubin, whose 1989 recording is on a modern copy of a Walter piano from 1795. Both pianists use a moderate rubato to punctuate the phrasing in the first two movements, and for expressive emphasis in the finale's second subject. Their carefully graded tempo fluctuations contrast with the much more sudden and exaggerated gear changes in Jos van Immerseel's 1983 recording on a Graf piano of 1824. Immerseel's performance lays more emphasis on the sonata's fantasy elements than any other recording in this survey. If the intensity and freedom of the performances by Bilson and Lubin recall somewhat the approach taken by Friedman, Lamond, and Schnabel, then Immerseel's reading might well bring to mind the criticisms of Liszt's early performances of the sonata (see page 49 above), in which freedom of expression was seen to distort the sonata's structure.

4

Quasi una fantasia?

We are used to making initial judgements about things from the names they bear. We have one set of expectations of a 'fantasy', another of a 'sonata'. . . We are satisfied if a second-rate talent shows that he has mastered the traditional range of forms, whereas with a first-rate talent we allow that he expand that range. Only a genius may reign freely.[1]

What, then, are we to make of Beethoven's title: *Sonata quasi una fantasia*? What might have prompted it, and what are the implications of its generic cross-fertilisation? Recent theories of genre suggest a number of avenues for the exploration of these questions.[2] Following the tenets of Russian formalist critics, studies could be made of the defining structural patterns associated with the classical sonata and eighteenth-century improvised fantasy, and of their relationship to one another in the fantasy-sonatas. Central to the formalist view of genres is the concept of a 'dominant', a defining element that categorises a genre and determines the function of other elements within it. Since Beethoven called these pieces *Sonata quasi una fantasia* rather than *Fantasia quasi una sonata*, the dominant generic strand seems self-evident. But the crucial ways in which sonata elements determine the functions of fantasy elements are not so straightforward.

Alternatively, the historical dimension of genre might be prioritised. Taking a lead from H. R. Jauss, a genre could be viewed as a historical 'family' of works. Jauss argued that the relationship between work and genre presents itself as 'a process of the continual founding and altering of horizons' in which some family characteristics remain invariable while others are modified or erased.[3] Thus the rider 'quasi una fantasia' might be seen as a token of Beethoven's evolving conception of the piano sonata, meaningful only when viewed against the background of his earlier sonatas and – more generally – in the context of generic trends in late eighteenth-century keyboard music as a whole.

Finally, an investigation of the significance of Beethoven's title might acknowledge a sociological aspect of genre. Accordingly a genre could be perceived to derive its meaning not only from the structures, stylistic features, and subject-matter of its constituent works, but from the willingness of a 'validating community' (for example composers, publishers, performers, and audiences) to sanction meaningful connections between titles, structures, styles, and contents.[4] In this way the meanings bestowed on genres can transcend taxonomic concerns and may be seen to be driven by the ideologies of the validating communities; they might encompass, for instance, aesthetic, polemical, or pedagogical issues. In the case of Op. 27, the mixture of sonata and fantasy in the title makes an aesthetic statement about the pieces, as well as positioning them within different formal categories of keyboard music. For a genre to operate at a given time and place, there must be a shared set of assumptions – a 'generic contract' – about its normative features. These affect both the production and reception of a work. When a composer chooses to write in a particular genre, creative decisions are made against the background of earlier works in the same genre. That background also focuses the responses of listeners: by creating a pattern for their expectations, it directs attention to the presence (or absence) of especially significant characteristics.[5] The more stable the shared assumptions, the more compelling the generic expectations. Genres such as the sonata and fantasy had relatively stable meanings for Beethoven's admirers in late-eighteenth-century Vienna. Although the originality of Beethoven's music constantly threatened to undermine the stability of generic contracts, his titles carry an obvious generic significance, all the more necessary in anchoring responses to works whose difficulty pushed his audience's understanding to its limit.[6] But if Beethoven's contemporaries knew what to expect of a sonata on the one hand and a fantasy on the other, what did it mean to them for a sonata to behave (and be judged) as though it were a fantasy?

Sonata *versus* fantasy

At the end of the eighteenth century the fundamental distinctions between the sonata and free fantasy stemmed from the premeditated, fixed condition of the former and the improvised, transitory existence of the latter. The styles and forms permissible in the sonata were somewhat prescribed by convention, but the fantasy was characterised by its greater formal freedom, its apparent lack of order and discipline in the working out of ideas, and the strangeness of effect that it allowed. While a sonata might contain between two and four 'closed' movements, fantasies were indivisible, though they could consist of several open-ended sections in different styles and forms.

Descriptions of sonatas from the late eighteenth century may be tested against the practice of surviving scores, but improvised fantasies – by their very nature – place the burden of evidence more squarely on theoretical discussions and eye-witness reports. Heinrich Christoph Koch, in his three major theoretical works, confined his comments to basic characteristics rather than discussing detailed points of style:

> In music the word Fantasy means . . . an extempore piece which is bound neither by a particular tempo nor by a particular metre in its sections; neither by a regular ordering [of its ideas], nor by a considered realisation; neither by a particular form, nor a strictly maintained character. Rather it is one in which the composer arranges the images of his imagination without an evident plan, or with a certain level of freedom, and thus sometimes in connected, at other times in quite loosely ordered phrases, and sometimes with particular broken chords.[7]

These comments summarise aspects of Carl Philipp Emanuel Bach's compendious discussion of improvisation in his *Versuch* (1753).[8] But in some respects Bach's account was more pragmatic than Koch's: he perceived the need to mediate between the performer's complete surrender to his imagination and the technical rigour through which the abandon should be expressed. His detailed comments elaborate three fundamental technical principles. First, compared with the sonata the fantasy allows greater freedom of modulation to keys remote from the tonic; paradoxically, while the exploration of distant keys seems to lack discipline, in comparison with the sonata's confined tonal range it demands a more thorough grasp of harmony. Second, Bach recommends that cadential articulation should be weak in a fantasy, since judiciously placed deceptive cadences can undermine an audience's expectations – one of the beauties of improvisation. Finally, an emphasis is placed on the importance of variety in figuration, because the unexpected is

Sonata	Fantasy
premeditated	improvised
multimovement	single movement
relative formal constraint	relative formal freedom
limited modulation permissible	free modulation permissible
unified affective character	varied affective character
clearly structured themes	ideas may be loosely structured
strong continuity ensures	ideas may be weakly connected,
comprehensibility	disjunctions are characteristic

Figure 4.1 A comparison of sonata and fantasy characteristics

characteristic of a fantasy, and 'the ear tires of unrelieved passage work'.[9]

Although eighteenth-century theorists discussed melodic variety and discontinuity in the fantasy, they did not comment on the details of suitable melodic styles, since to do so would hardly have been in the spirit of the genre. Melody was the prime indicator of subjectivity in the improvised fantasy because – above all other musical parameters – it was considered to represent best the performer's unfettered imagination. Nevertheless, from eye-witness reports it can be surmised that Beethoven's improvisations contained four basic melodic styles: elaborate virtuoso figuration; irregular melodies suggesting recitative style; cantabile melodies analogous to aria styles; and strict contrapuntal style. The free, highly nuanced qualities of the first two styles offer a sharp contrast with the sweeping 'symphonic' style of Beethoven's sonatas from the 1790s.[10] And, on the evidence of the Op. 27 sonatas, the strict contrapuntal style was only one of several 'archaic' styles (redolent of the Baroque) which Beethoven could deploy in his improvisations.

In summary, a comparison of sonata and fantasy characteristics, as decribed by eighteenth-century theorists, is outlined in Figure 4.1.

Against this pure generic background the contrast between the sonata and fantasy was blurred by the improvised ornamentation of composed music in performance; by a distinction between improvised and notated fantasies; and by a gradual rapprochement of sonata and fantasy styles generally in instrumental music during the last decades of the eighteenth century. In an era which had no clear conception of musical interpretation in a twentieth-century sense, ornamentation represented the creative (as opposed to recreative) aspect of performing. The opportunity for spontaneity in a premeditated context allowed performers to recapture the expressive immediacy of the fantasy. At its highest level, this performing style can be glimpsed in the profusely ornamented version of the Adagio in the first edition of Mozart's Sonata in F K.332/300k (Artaria, 1784) which dramatically heightens the pathetic sensibility of the simpler version in Mozart's autograph score. On the other hand, the practice of fixing improvisations in musical notation seems to have inhibited the wilder excesses of musical fantasy, since the act of writing compromised spontaneity and was necessarily cramped by the limitations of the notational system. Theorists recognised such a distinction between free (improvised) and strict (notated) fantasies. Koch wrote that the notated fantasy 'generally comes a step closer to the methodical and regulated aspects of orderly elaborated pieces than [a fantasy] which is immediately transferred to the instrument ex tempore'.[11] And for Daniel Gottlob Türk a strict fantasy was one 'in which metre is fundamental, in which there is a greater adherence to the laws of modulation, and in which a greater unity is observed'.[12] The strict fantasy, while retaining the connotations of the free fantasy in terms of violence of expression, strangeness of effect and formal freedom, shared with the sonata a more prescribed tonal and metrical framework. Such pieces might be perceived as compositions in the style of a fantasy, or even pieces about improvising, rather than as transcriptions of actual improvisations. In this way the fantasy became a source of stereotypical musical devices which could be borrowed as topics for discourse in other genres.

This process was part of a larger historical trend that profoundly affected instrumental styles towards the end of the eighteenth century. Peter Schleuning has described how the free fantasy lost its generic autonomy at this time due in part to the infiltration of sonata and fantasy characteristics in all instrumental genres.[13] Already in the later music of Haydn and Mozart the distinction between 'free' and 'structured' styles was beginning to disintegrate: notated fantasies acquired formal features of the sonata, and fantasy tropes played an increasingly important role in sonatas, symphonies, and concertos. The infection of sonatas by fantasy tropes took place at all levels of organisation. It affected the type

| K.282/189g | Adagio | Minuets 1 and 2 | Allegro |
| K.331/300i | Andante grazioso | Menuet and Trio | [Rondo] Alla Turca. Allegretto |

Figure 4.2 Unconventional formal patterns in Mozart Sonatas

and distribution of movements and the tonal relationships between them. Haydn's late piano trios, string quartets and symphonies are especially adventurous in this respect: movements are elided,[14] the structural tonic–dominant relationship is undermined by an abundance of relationships between keys a third apart,[15] and there is a marked increase in forms that evolve *sui generis*.[16] Such mixing of styles also took place in keyboard music. Several sonatas by Haydn and Mozart anticipate the integration of sonata and fantasy elements in Beethoven's Op. 27. Haydn's A major Sonata Hob. XVI:30 (1774) consists of three movements – Allegro, Adagio, and Tempo di Menuet – that play continuously, sharing motives and structural features.[17] Similarly a D major Sonata from 1780 (Hob. XVI:37) runs together its second and third movements: an improvisatory Largo e sostenuto and a rondo finale. Like Beethoven's Op. 27 sonatas, two of Mozart's sonatas eschew an opening sonata Allegro, beginning instead with slow movements, continuing with triple-time dance movements, and ending more conventionally with fast movements in either sonata or rondo forms (see Figure 4.2). Moreover, K.331/300i is, like the 'Moonlight' Sonata, monotonal (all its movements are in A); but Mozart (unlike Beethoven) does not call for individual movements to be run into one another.

At a more detailed level, fantasy was one of many stylistic topics that could characterise a movement or section, or which might be deployed along with other topics to articulate the tonal contrasts of sonata form. The instability inherent in the fantasy style made it an ideal topic for slow introductions, transitions, and development sections.[18] In slow introductions the varied character and loose connections between themes formed an effective foil to the strongly connected themes and powerful teleological drive of the following sonata Allegro. This is a rhetorical plan that Beethoven expanded in the Op. 27 sonatas: in each of them a sonata-like finale emerges from earlier movements in which fantasy elements predominate. In transitions and development sections too the free modulation and strangeness of effect typical of the fantasy allowed composers boldly to expand the range and scope of their music. This is especially evident in the increasing use (and acceptability) of dissonant prolongations, such as emphases on augmented sixths and diminished sevenths, the tendency to build tension by withholding their resolution, and – in extreme cases – sudden and wild modulations. Conversely, notated fantasies increasingly resembled more structured genres in both form and rhetoric. Many critics have pointed out that Haydn's keyboard Fantasy in C (Hob. XVII:4, 1789) is a tautly structured rondo which – its wild modulations apart – displays little more gestural anarchy than those 'composed' pieces in which he indulges his natural *Willkür*.[19] Mozart's two keyboard fantasies from his Vienna years mix stable 'structured' passages with free improvisatory and modulating sections.[20] Their use of thematic reprise is also symptomatic of a 'composed' style: in the C minor Fantasy K.475 the opening sections's themes (bars 1–25) return at the end of the piece in bars 161–76, and the D minor Fantasy fragment K.397/385g contains large-scale repetition. A similar trend emerges in the extant authentic cadenzas for Mozart's piano concertos. Those for the Salzburg concertos (written in the 1770s) conform to the style of the mid–century free fantasy. But those for the Viennese concertos are closer in style to 'composed' fantasies: their immaculate pacing, careful manipulation of register and texture, and their chromatic subtlety simulate improvisation in a thoroughly premeditated way. Nevertheless, as William Kinderman has observed, Mozart's cadenzas turn musical spontaneity itself into a discursive topic.[21] Perhaps the clearest indication of the convergence of sonata and fantasy styles in the classical period comes from Mozart's juxtaposition of his C minor Fantasy (K.475) and Sonata (K.457) in the first edition by Artaria (1785). The process of integration had advanced so far by the mid-1780s that, rather than revealing stark stylistic contrasts, the two works seem to offer complementary perspectives on a single style.

As mentioned in chapter 2, the dialectic between the expressive immediacy of fantasy style and the structural coherence of sonata style reached an unprecedented level of synthesis in Beethoven's early music. At the same time, however, the genres of fantasy and sonata diverged anew at the beginning of the nineteenth century with the emergence of the so-called 'salon' fantasy. This was a popular genre that lacked the intellectual and aesthetic pretensions of the eighteenth-century free fantasy. It mixed virtuoso figuration with pot-pourris, variations, and contrapuntal elaborations of popular songs and arias. Beethoven's two notated fantasies (Opp. 77 and 80) belong to this category (as, at a more exalted level, does the finale of the ninth symphony), though their closing variations are based on original themes.[22] Clearly the term 'fantasy' had acquired a different set of connotations for the composer by the second decade of the century, and this might partly explain why, despite the striking rhapsodic styles and formal experiments of the late sonatas, none of them was called *Sonata quasi una fantasia*. The Op. 27 sonatas therefore appear to be situated on the cusp of a powerful historical trend in serious German instrumental music. In comparison with the classical repertoire, all Beethoven's early sonatas are, in a sense, 'quasi una fantasia', but only in Op. 27 did his violation of classical sonata decorum become so acute that it needed to be signalled with the addendum.[23] And generic expectations of 'fantasy' had not yet sufficiently evolved in the direction of popular salon fantasies to make the rider redundant, or even misleading.[24]

Sonata as fantasy

Given that sonata and fantasy were separate genres, what did it mean for Beethoven's contemporaries to judge a sonata *as if* it were a fantasy? Critiques of sonatas in the late eighteenth century tended to emphasise formal qualities associated with beauty: well-orderedness, coherence, comprehensibility. Even reviews of Beethoven's early sonatas, which comment on the music's fantastic aspect, do so within the context of sonata-like coherence and comprehensibility.[25] But fantasies elicited a different response, in which priority was given to the language of feeling rather than the language of form, and in which the imagery of the sublime was constantly evoked. This is exemplified in Ignaz von Seyfried's description of Beethoven improvising in the early 1790s:

> In his improvisations . . . Beethoven did not deny his tendency towards the mysterious and gloomy. When once he began to revel in the infinite world of tones, he was transported above all earthly things; his spirit had burst all restricting bonds, shaken off the yoke of servitude, and soared triumphantly and jubilantly into the luminous spaces of the higher ether.

Now his playing tore along like a wildly foaming cataract, and the conjurer constrained his instrument to an utterance so forceful that the stoutest structure was scarcely able to withstand it; and anon he sank down exhausted, exhaling gentle plaints, dissolving in melancholy. Again the spirit would soar aloft, triumphing over earthly sufferings, turn its glance upward in reverent sounds and find rest and comfort on the innocent bosom of holy nature. But who shall sound the depths of the sea? It was the mystical Sanskrit language whose hieroglyphs can be read only by the initiated.[26]

In contrast to contemporaneous technical discussions of the fantasy, which highlighted lack of order, Seyfried – in common with other eye-witnesses of Beethoven's playing – unified the fantasy by construing it as a narrative of affective states. Despite the impossibility of attributing a specific meaning to the piece ('the mystical Sanskrit language'), he articulates the succession of affects in terms of contrasting levels: melancholy depths, transcendental heights, and an energetic medium. Given the intensified sensibility, it is perhaps not surprising that everyday placidity is conspicuous by its absence. Seyfried was writing some time after the event, and his description appears idealised, striving to reflect in the tone of his prose the fantasy of the improvisation itself.[27] But less self-conscious responses to Beethoven's improvisations were equally sentimental. Czerny recorded an occasion when 'hardly any eye remained dry, while many broke into loud sobs'.[28]

What does this sentimental reaction tell us about the relationship between Beethoven and his audience? In her study of sensibility in eighteenth-century literature, Janet Todd describes the status of the poet in sentimental criticism:

> Like poetry, the idea of the poet caused sentimental critics to grow rhapsodical. Severed from long apprenticeship to rules and styles, the artist became demystified into a superior sensibility, a kind of emotional vibrator. [The critic John] Dennis saw [the poet's] greatness in his capacity to feel enthusiastic passion and in his emotional distinction from others; Shaftesbury considered him as imitating in his art the divine act of creation itself . . . A proper response to poetry was not comparison and criticism but wonder and complete surrender.[29]

For Beethoven's contemporaries, to witness one of his improvisations was akin to experiencing a revelation of the composer's superior sensibility, a privileged glimpse of the 'authentic' artist. According to Baron de

Trémont 'those who had been unable to hear him improvise freely had only an incomplete knowledge of the entire depth and power of his genius'.[30] And Johann Schenk made a similar point in more vivid detail, reporting how, in an improvisation, Beethoven's genius 'revealed . . . its deeply expressive portrait of the soul' when the composer 'abandoned all his power to the magic of his sounds, and with the fire of youth he began boldly to express violent passions in more distant keys'.[31] But if the sentimental power of fantasy was liberating, it also had a more dangerous side. The 'conjurer' could be taken over by his own magic. In *Herzen-ergiessungen eines kunstliebenden Klosterbruders* (1797), Wackenroder described how the fictitious composer Berlinger, lacking the technique needed to communicate his ideas effectively, was destroyed by his boundless fantasy and extreme sensitivity.[32] As Dahlhaus commented, a number of seminal early Romantic German writers, including Jean Paul Richter and Wackenroder, expressed scepticism about the *furor poeticus* (poetic frenzy), 'convinced that the idea that flashes upon the poet in his ecstasy must be seized and carried over into a state of sobriety if it is to assume firm and lasting form'.[33] In this light, the hybrid genre of the sonata *quasi una fantasia* might be perceived as an attempt to represent the *furor poeticus* within the fixed framework of the sonata. The danger and intensity of the fantasy could be experienced through the safety of the well-ordered sonata, while retaining the revelatory qualities of the genuine article. Thus, with his hybrid title, Beethoven was demanding that the Op. 27 sonatas be judged according to an unconventional set of criteria in which sentiment, as much as formal beauty, plays a role. For the few who had been privileged to hear Beethoven improvise, the concept of the sonata-as-fantasy must have been like a memento of those occasions. And for performers, the Op. 27 sonatas gave the opportunity of entering into a closer communion (to extend the mystical language of contemporaneous commentators) with the essence of Beethoven's genius.

Sentimental views of Beethoven's artistic powers were central to his growing success during his first decade in Vienna. Obscure, bizarre, and challenging aspects of his music could be turned from a potential disadvantage with his audience to an advantage by appealing to the revelatory qualities of his originality. Nikolaus Zmeskall noted that 'hearers not only accustomed themselves to the striking and original qualities of the master but grasped his spirit and strove for the *high privilege* of understanding him'.[34] To have the 'high privilege' of understanding Beethoven's unconventional musical language was to become an 'initiate' of 'the mystical Sanskrit language' (Seyfried) and to attain a more complete 'knowledge of the entire depth and power of his genius' (Trémont). The significance of the title *Sonata quasi una fantasia* thus transcends local matters of form and style. It is a significant marker in Beethoven's successful attempt to win a unique reputation with his patrons and public. By demanding that they judge his sonatas according to the criteria reserved for fantasies, the composer was asserting his autonomy from the vagaries of popular taste, and his compositional experiments in the following years are unthinkable without the success of this declaration. In this way the Op. 27 sonatas may be seen to form a keystone in the forging of Beethoven's artistic identity.

5

The design of the Op. 27 sonatas

Both Op. 27 sonatas outline a gradual progression from 'static' circular structures to dynamic linear processes; from 'content-based' ambiguous forms to finales that can be understood against normative models like sonata form and rondo. While all but one of their movements are structurally self-sufficient and can be perceived as discrete segments, Beethoven asks for them to be run together in performance to give the impression of a continuous whole. Structurally this integration is supported by the large tonal patterns governing each work: C♯ is the tonic for all three movements in the second sonata; and the first sonata's movements, though encompassing a wider tonal range, are enmeshed together by an interlocking series of tonics (bracketed in Figure 5.1).

An impression of continuity is reinforced at a more detailed level by the cohesive actions of motivic integration and gestural recall: ideas from the opening movements return transformed in the dynamic context of the finales. Yet from moment to moment the musical continuity is often threatened by Beethoven's allusions to musical spontaneity. The threat comes to the fore most obviously in cadenza-like passages and in disjunctions of tonality, tempo, idea, register, and texture. In this respect some critics have detected a stronger element of the fantastic in the E♭ sonata than in the 'Moonlight': while the element of *Willkür* is

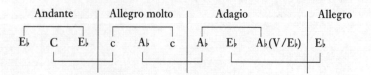

Figure 5.1 Tonal integration in Op. 27 no. 1

perhaps less prominent in the second sonata, Czerny regarded the first as a paragon among strictly composed fantasies.[1]

No. 1 in E♭

Andante – Allegro – Andante

In keeping with the fantasy style the first movement is a content-based form. It cannot be understood in terms of any one formal archetype but springs *sui generis* from its materials. Nevertheless, it is informed in subtle ways by at least three different formal models (see Figure 5.2). Rondo is suggested by the manner in which varied reprises of the theme alternate with contrasting episodes. But these episodes may themselves be regarded as more heavily disguised variations of the opening theme. Variation processes may thus be seen to control the entire movement, but the larger *formal* arrangement of the variations has little in common with the typical layout of classical variation sets. And overlying these patterns, the movement's tempo and key changes point to a ternary design. For the sake of clarity Figure 5.2 has oversimplified the role of these archetypes: in reality Beethoven's fantasy-like exploration of the opening ideas sets up richly ambiguous patterns.

Tempo	Andante			Allegro	Andante	
Key	E♭			C	E♭	
bars	1–8	9–20	21–36	37–62	63–78	79–86
Rondo	A¹	B	A²	C	A³	Coda
Variations	Theme	Var 1	Var 2	Var 3	Var 4	Coda
Ternary	A¹			B	A²	Coda

Figure 5.2 Formal stereotypes informing the first movement

Theme (bars 1–8)

In comparison with the dynamic, arresting gestures that open Beethoven's earlier sonatas, the start of this movement is uncharacteristically understated, placid, and – above all – preoccupied with short-term closure: strong perfect cadences in E♭ occur at the end of every four bars. Critics for whom the theme is 'trivial' or even 'unworthy of Beethoven' have perhaps concentrated too much on the melody and not

Example 5.1 Op. 27/1/i bars 1–4

enough on the interplay between the treble and bass. But it cannot be denied that the theme is set within severe harmonic and rhythmic restrictions: the pattern of repeated ♩ ♩ ♩ rhythms and the circling between I and V is broken only at the cadence in bars 7–8. Inevitably such repetitions divert attention away from the melody towards the underlying harmonies, but two melodic details do prove significant in the long-term unfolding of the piece. Thirds play a prominent role in the first phrase, not only in the initial fall $b\flat^1$–g^1 in the first bar, but also in the gradual descent through g^1–f^1–$e\flat^1$ in an inner voice in bars 1–4 (Example 5.1). Together with the dactyls, these motives play a significant role in binding together the various sections of the sonata. In the second phrase the most important melodic detail is the apex of the broken V^7 chord on $a\flat^2$ in bar 7. This pitch remains a fixed point of articulation in the subsequent variations (see, for instance, bars 14 and 62) and also appears at important formal points much later in the sonata (for example, the end of the Adagio con espressione and at the climax of the finale).

Rondo
On the surface, the first movement's different sections are articulated by changing musical emphases. While bars 1–8 focus attention on the harmony, sentimental melody takes centre stage in the first episode (bars 9–16). Details from the opening are freely re-interpreted: greater rhythmic variety springs from the head-motive, the melodic space between g^1 and $b\flat^1$ is filled over two bars (bars 9–10) instead of one, and the theme's left-hand semiquavers reappear only in the last two bars. A more dramatic shift marks the start of the second episode in bar 37, with changes of key, tempo and style. If the first episode takes its starting point from the right hand in bars 1–8, then the second episode's semiquaver patterns seem to refer back to the accompanying bass line. Both episodes stand out from the refrain with their expanded harmonic range. In the

context of the movement's hitherto limited harmonic vocabulary the C major chord in bar 13 has an expressive weight far in excess of its structural importance as a chromatic passing chord. It is indeed the single most memorable sound in the first episode. No doubt the unconventional use of C major as a subsidiary tonality in the Allegro episode springs from Beethoven fantastically seizing on this earlier detail and elevating its structural significance.

Variations

Cutting across this episodic form, however, is a series of subtle transformations of the opening theme's harmonic structure. Figure 5.3 compares the harmonic pattern of bars 1–4 with the parallel sections of the 'episodic' variations. As the arrows indicate, the V 'pillar' is pushed progressively later in each section, until it reaches the double bar in the Allegro (bar 44).

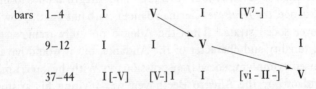

Figure 5.3 Harmonic transformations in the first section of the theme

A more complex transformation affects the second part of the theme in the episodes (see Figure 5.4). In the theme a two-bar V^7 is interrupted at bar 7 and I is reached after a rapid circle of fifths in bars 7–8. The same circle of fifths (with vi changed to VI) is extended to cover the whole of the phrase in the first episode (bars 13–16). Finally, there is a double take on this pattern in the Allegro. The G^7 chord in bars 53–6 has two functions: it acts locally as V^7/C (functionally analogous to the V^7 in bar 5) but it also initiates a further expansion of the circle of fifths, returning the music to $V/E\flat$ in preparation for the closing Andante.

Ternary form

The single most important formal event in the first movement is the interruption of the E♭ Andante by a C major Allegro in $\frac{6}{8}$ time. If eyewitness reports are to be believed such sudden unexpected reversals

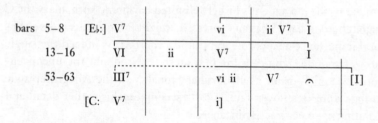

Figure 5.4 Harmonic transformations in the second section of the theme

were typical in Beethoven's improvisations, so the strategy may be taken as another token of the fantasy style here. But the contrasts involved would have carried more specific stylistic connotations for Beethoven's contemporaries. The Andante's rhythmic patterns refer unmistakably to the gavotte: a dance which in the late eighteenth century was associated with the 'high style' and the aristocracy.[2] The Allegro alludes to another type of dance, the *Deutsche* (German dance), with links to the 'low style' and lower social strata.[3] Thus the Allegro not only trangresses the tempo, tonality and character of the Andante, but it would have been recognised as implying social transgression too. With the interruption of the Andante by the Allegro Beethoven was inviting his aristocratic patrons to confront the claims of two rival value systems. On the one hand the sentimental Andante represents their elitism; on the other, the energetic Allegro represents middle- or even low-brow culture. Since the E♭ Andante is seen to overcome the Allegro, there can be no doubt whose values are seen to prevail. But the outcome is provisional: in each of the subsequent movements Beethoven presents his 'audience' with a similar choice between their own aesthetic values and alternatives. Thus the integration of the separate movements into an indivisible fantasy-sonata goes beyond form and structure to involve the very aesthetic premises of the genre.

Allegro molto e vivace

This ternary-form movement is a Scherzo and Trio in all but name (see Figure 5.5 for a formal breakdown). In common with many of Beethoven's scherzi, the rhythmic details of each bar are relatively unimportant in comparison with the grouping of bars into larger units

'Scherzo'	A¹	bars	1–17	c–g
	B		18–24	V/f–c
	A²		25–41	c
'Trio'	C		42–55	A♭–E♭
	D		56–73	E♭⁷–A♭
'Scherzo'	A¹		73–104	c–g
	B		105–12	V/f–c
	A²		113–27	c
Coda			128–40	C

Figure 5.5 Formal outline of Allegro molto e vivace

Example 5.2 Op. 27/1/ii Hypermetrical structure

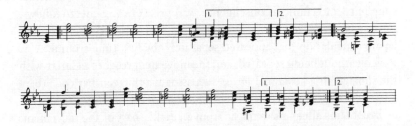

('hypermeters'). Its four-bar hypermeters are shown in Example 5.2, an outline in which each crotchet represents a bar of Beethoven's score. As several critics have noted, bar 1 must be understood as an upbeat to the first main metrical accent at bar 2, but the subsequent grouping is completely regular.

The Scherzo is based on an old cliché: the descending chromatic bass (covering the interval C to G here). During the seventeenth and eighteenth centuries this figure was taken to represent feelings of sadness or suffering, an expressive character that is intensified by Beethoven's dissonant modifications to the treble in A² (giving rise to 7–6 suspensions and diminished seventh chords). Most of its famous Baroque manifestations (such as 'When I am laid in earth' from Purcell's *Dido and Aeneas*, and the 'Crucifixus' of Bach's Mass in B minor) are variations on a ground, whose bass patterns are circular and potentially endless. However, Beethoven pointedly places the figure in a modern context by constructing a classical antecedent-consequent relationship between A¹ (ending on v) and A² (ending on i). For the connoisseurs among his supporters this marriage of ancient and modern must have made a highly significant contrast with the Trio's modern, comic scherzando style.

Beethoven's more knowledgeable contemporaries might have recognised in the Trio several similarities with minuets from Haydn's most recent string quartets. Its harmonic stasis, iambic ostinato, and off-beat arpeggios all recall the Menuet: Presto of Op. 76 no. 6 in E♭ (written in 1796 or 1797 and published in Vienna in December 1799) and the Trio of Op. 77 no. 1 in G (written 1799, published around the same time as Beethoven's Op. 27 in 1802). But not even Haydn dared pare his material to the minimalist levels Beethoven achieves here. Since the Trio's harmonic structure owes much to the opening theme of the preceding Andante it may be perceived as yet another variation, though the thinness of its material falls beyond the first movement's sentimental simplicity into comic inconsequence. A reprise of the Scherzo follows. Beethoven writes out a varied repeat of A^1, combining the staccato and legato articulation that appeared separately the first time around. A^2 is varied without being repeated, and the movement reaches a climax with the sonata's first sustained *fortissimo* passage: a thirteen-bar coda (bars 128–40) comprising an extended *tierce de Picardie*. Characteristically, the coda contains allusions to music from an earlier part of the movement: the motion of the inner voice (b♭–a♭–g) in bars 130–2 and 134–6 brings back the shape of the treble line in **B** (bars 17b–22).

Thus in this movement Beethoven again juxtaposes two very different styles representing contrasting values: the Scherzo exhibits old-fashioned virtues, its ideas are serious and substantial; the Trio exemplifies the most insubstantial aspects of the modern style, with athematic jesting and mockery. And once more, with the Scherzo's reprise, the values most closely associated with Beethoven's connoisseur patrons win through.

Adagio con espressione

Beethoven's admirers often praised the particular eloquence of his Adagio playing, and he was famed for the type of elevated lyricism which is given voice in this Adagio con espressione. Leonard Ratner has noted that one of the main functions of the high sentimental style in musical classicism was 'to celebrate authority' in operas.[4] In this movement the

A^1	1–8	A♭
B	9–16	E♭
A^2	17–24	A♭
Eingang	24–6	A♭–V/E♭

Figure 5.6 Formal outline of Adagio con espressione

style may be taken to exemplify the authority of the artist's sentiments and implicitly to uphold the social authority of Beethoven's aristocratic patrons. In this way it engages with the play of contrasting values found in the first two movements. Ratner has characterised the high sentimental style as having a 'grand manner', 'sense of elevation', and 'well-turned' melodies.[5] Here these qualities are embodied in the stately tempo and sonorous textures, the careful integration of expressive details into the broad sweep of its melodies (especially the chromatic *sospirando* figures in its central section), and the density of expression marks so typical of musical pathos. Its ornate melody carries the main burden of expression, but – in what may be a subtle allusion to improvisatory practices – the underlying harmony of its outer sections is unusually simple.[6]

Like the first two movements, the Adagio is in a three-part form (Figure 5.6). In keeping with the thematic integration typical of the fantasy style, A^1 contains subtle allusions to the sonata's opening theme, with its initial emphasis on I (bars 1–4), later emphasis on V^7 (bars 5–8), and descent from $\hat{3}$ to $\hat{1}$ (c¹–a♭) in the first two bars. B abruptly tonicises E♭ and provides a thematic and rhetorical contrast to the first section. The bass is more mobile here and chords appear in less stable positions. A first attempt to cadence is thwarted by an interruption at bar 12; the second attempt (made beneath syncopated sighing figures in bars 13–16) is successful. But as soon as E♭ has been anchored with a perfect cadence it turns into V/A♭ and cadences into a varied reprise of the first theme (A^2). Beethoven's treatment of the theme recalls Seyfried's description of the the composer's use of contrasting registers in improvisations (see pp. 62–3). In A^1 the theme begins in a sonorous tenor register and ascends through an octave; in A^2 it starts an octave higher and ultimately rises to the top of the keyboard by the closing cadence in bars 23–4. The melodic emphasis on e♭³ in these bars gently compromises the finality of the cadence, and the movement dissolves into a fantasy-style *Eingang*, modulating to V/E♭ to introduce the following Allegro vivace. Although many commentators have regarded the Adagio as an autonomous movement, there are good grounds for thinking of it as part of a composite movement, an introduction to what follows: since it does not close strongly in A♭ major it is not structurally self-sufficient; it is relatively brief; and it is further integrated with the Allegro near the end of the sonata. Moreover a small detail of the first edition supports this view: when the Adagio's main theme returns towards the end of the sonata it is marked 'Tempo I'.

Allegro vivace

Finally the earlier movements' static forms give way to the linear processes of a sonata-rondo form in which the central episode takes on characteristics of a development, and the last episode acts as a recapitulation and tonal resolution of the first episode (see Figure 5.7).

Within the new dynamic flux of the finale old ideas reappear. Most obviously the rondo's refrain transforms the sonata's opening theme (see Example 5.3). While some aspects of the original's symmetrical phrasing are retained, the refrain's rhythmic asymmetries and wide

'Exposition'	*Refrain 1*			
	A	bars	1–8	E♭ (I)
	B		9–24	V–I
	Episode 1			
	Transition		25–35	E♭–B♭
	Secondary ideas		35–56	V/B♭
	Closing theme / Retransition		56–81	B♭–V/E♭
'Development'	*Refrain 2*		82–105	E♭–e♭–V/G♭
	Episode 2			
	Fugato		106–31	G♭–b♭
	Retransition		131–66	b♭–V/E♭
'Recapitulation'	*Refrain 3*		167–90	E♭
	Episode 3		191–240	E♭
Coda			240–85	E♭

Figure 5.7 Formal outline of Allegro vivace

Example 5.3 Op. 27/1 Themes of the first and last movements

registral range release symphonic energies that were only latent in the opening Andante. Affective details are no longer of primary importance: they are now subsidiary to the long-term tonal processes that underpin them.

A modulating transition section begins in bar 25. Characteristically Beethoven pushes the music towards V/V very rapidly by obsessively repeating the refrain's head-motive on different degrees of the scale. But having achieved its short-term harmonic goal the music now seems to lose its way. Instead of cadencing into B♭ for the second subject, it takes a much more extended, circuitous route towards V. For eight bars the bass remains stuck on a pedal f^1 while the treble moves in chromatic circles around $b♭^1$ (bars 36–43). The bass is finally dislodged in bar 44, but its subsequent chromatic ascent seems to take the music still further away from its harmonic goal, moving instead to A♭ at bar 48. It takes a descending chromatic *excursus* (bars 50ff.) to finally reach the expected goal of B♭ in bar 56, an achievement celebrated with fanfares in the next bars. Every element of the final theme signifies musical closure: its harmonic stability (over a B♭ pedal), its reassertion of metrical periodicity after the aperiodic *Fortspinnung* of the preceding passage, and finally its climactic ascent to the very top of the instrument's range (f^3) and its conclusive reference to the end of the refrain (the rising third g^2–a^2–$b♭^2$ in bar 63 onwards). Yet, despite all these tokens of closure, *actual* closure is thwarted. The music's rhythmic momentum sweeps on unchecked, and instead of bringing it to a stop Beethoven introduces A♭ (bar 72) and C♭

(bar 74), changing the function of B♭ from local I to V/E♭, and leading to a reprise of the refrain at bar 82.

The refrain takes a new turn at bar 99, darkening to E♭ minor and thence to its relative major (G♭) at bar 106, where a fugato breaks out. Its subject and countersubject are based on the beginning of the refrain. An exchange of subject – answer – subject keeps the music in G♭ during bars 106–15, then an episode leads to a bass statement of the subject in B♭ minor at bar 118. A further episode of two-part imitation whirls through a circle of fifths, but returns to its tonal starting-point at bar 131. B♭ minor is anchored by rather over-emphatic cadences in bars 131–9, concluding the first part of the episode. A retransition to the refrain follows. In a progression that mirrors the overall tonal design of the first three movements, the treble falls through a series of thirds ($b♭^2$–$g♭^2$–$e♭^2$) in bars 139–54, underpinned by fragments of the secondary ideas. The treble's broad E♭ minor arpeggio is answered in bars 155–66 by a broken chord of V (d^2–f^2–$b♭^2$). This resolves into I at bar 167.

Beethoven launches the recapitulation with another reprise of the refrain (bars 167–90). This is unchanged until bar 183 where – in another obvious echo of the first movement – the two-part texture is inverted (compare with the Andante, bars 67–70 and 75–8). To keep the music in E♭ the transition is modified, and from bar 200 the exposition's second group of themes is transposed into the tonic. Characteristically Beethoven introduces the coda by mirroring the join between the exposition and development. Thus the fanfare theme is prevented from closing properly by the addition of $d♭^1$ in bar 240, though its pull towards the subdominant (A♭) is resisted. Instead the bass rises chromatically, leading through a series of chromatic chords before reaching a dominant seventh in bar 246. Such a chromatic intensification is a sure sign of impending climax, and Beethoven proceeds to unleash the most brilliant climax of the sonata, stopping the music dead in its tracks at a mighty V^7 chord in bar 255. In an improvisation this strategy would be thrilling. The chord demands resolution: what will happen next? A glittering apotheosis of the refrain? A witty punchline, like the end of the Seventh Symphony's Scherzo? Merely by provoking these questions Beethoven reintroduces the issue of spontaneity as a topic for musical discourse. He answers the questions with yet another sudden reversal of tone. The goal of the movement (and hence of the sonata) is not the brilliant style but a

Example 5.4 Op. 27/1 Melodic complementarity

return to elevated sentiment with a reprise of the closing section from the Adagio con espressione, now in E♭. Yet even this does not have the last word. Mirroring its earlier appearance, the theme dissolves into a fantasy-style *Eingang*, and introduces a short concluding Presto. Evoking for a last time the improvisatory technique of seizing upon an apparently insignificant detail, Beethoven muses on the closing interval of the *Eingang* (a♭–f) and repeats falling thirds obsessively in the Presto.[7]

Any analysis concerned with the music's structural integrity is duty bound to attempt to explain why Beethoven reprised the Adagio at bar 256. There is no shortage of reasons to hand: the reprise resolves the structural dissonance of the theme's earlier appearance in A♭; its head-motive can be construed as a melodic complement to the rondo's opening idea (Example 5.4);[8] and it has the necessary harmonic stability to ground the the tonic, thus securing proper closure. Beyond these structural issues there are sound generic reasons for the composer's strategy. It further enhances the integration of the Adagio and the Allegro, drawing attention to a formal characteristic of the fantasy. Perhaps more significantly it re-asserts the authority of a superior sensibility at the sonata's climax. But if the reprise of the Adagio is designed to close the sonata's tonal structure and leave a lasting impression of the high style then it singularly fails to achieve either aim. Despite repeated perfect cadences in bars 262–4 the treble ornamentation increases tension rather than resolving it. The sonata's expressive intensity reaches its apogee in the questioning dominant ninths of bars 264–5; that they should be answered (and the sonata closed) by the Presto's comic style is, to say the least, incongruous.[9]

It is tempting to believe that such structural explanations miss the the point: for all its musical logic the coda gives the overwhelming impression of being an arbitrary succession of ideas. Throughout the sonata opposing qualities have jostled for supremacy. The values of Beethoven's elite audience and their sentimental view of the artist's superior sensibility have constantly prevailed. In the first movement the gavotte has overcome the German dance; in the second, serious Baroque topics have obliterated the trio's flippant comedy; and the finale's dramatic linearity has seemingly found its fulfilment in a triumphant return to the high sensibility of the Adagio. But the Presto so suddenly and so utterly subverts this pattern that it invites an ironic understanding of the coda as a whole. If the sonata's true goal is the comic Presto then the reprise of the Adagio must be regarded as a last-minute ironic interpolation. If, on the other hand, the reprise of the Adagio is the real goal, reinforcing the dominant value system of the sonata as a whole, then the Presto must be an ironic appendix. But which of them is ironic? It is perhaps in this unresolvable issue that the heart of this particular sonata-as-fantasy resides.

No. 2 in C♯ minor ('Moonlight')

Adagio sostenuto

Like Hamlet's soliloquy on suicide this movement has become such an icon in the popular imagination that its context has almost ceased to signify. Yet to ignore the stylistic tradition from which it springs and its place within the sonata as a whole is to disregard a wide range of possiblities in the music's function and meaning. The Adagio sostenuto belongs to a long tradition of *Trauermusik* (mourning music). A set of elaborate, formal musical ideas and devices was developed in the seventeenth and eighteenth centuries to depict reactions to death and suffering. Beethoven uses a whole collection of these devices in this movement: the *Lament* bass, melodic shapes derived from plainchant, repetitive accompaniment figures, and chromatic figures.[10] But in contrast to the formality of the tradition, Beethoven fashions his materials with an unprecedented flexibility. Chant was a rich repository of melodic ideas for eighteenth-century composers, and was thought particularly suitable for music in serious styles, or which played with forms from earlier generations. Famous examples of its use in the classical era include Haydn's quotation of a chant associated with the Lamentations of Jeremiah in his Symphony no. 26, Mozart's use of the psalm chant *tonus peregrinus* in his Masonic Funeral Music, and the Requiem. At the outset of

Example 5.5 (a). Lamentatio: 1st Psalm Tone (transposed) (b). Tonus peregrinus (transposed) (c). Beethoven Op. 27/2/i bars 5–9

the C♯ minor Sonata Beethoven alludes to both these chants, though he stops short of actual quotation (Example 5.5). The ecclesiastical undertone is subtly enhanced by the melody's chorale-like groupings in the first part of the movement. Equally pertinent to the mourning topic is the monotone and dotted anacrusis that characterises many of the melodic phrases. In this context the monotone inevitably recalls the tolling of a bell, and the dotted anacrusis recalls the *Marcia sulla morte d'un eroe* from the Sonata in A♭ Op. 26, and anticipates the main theme of the 'Eroica' Symphony's *Marcia funebre*. The chromatic elements and modal changes that permeate the movement belong to a much older category of figures representing mourning in music: seventeenth-century rhetorical figures like *pathopoeia* and *passus duriusculus* (both terms for dissonant chromatic steps that express affections like sadness, fear and terror), and *mutatio toni* (the sudden shifting of tone or mode for expressive reasons). A further network of allusions is created by the accompaniment's triplets. Edward J. Dent noted their similarity to the music that accompanies the death of the Commendatore in the *Introduzione* to Act 1 of Mozart's *Don Giovanni* (1787);[11] and they anticipate the *maggiore* section of the funeral march in the 'Eroica'. In summary, the Adagio sostenuto might well be regarded as a highly original and personal essay on mourning and loss.

bars	1–23	23–41	42–60	60–69
	Exposition	'Development'	Recapitulation	Coda

Figure 5.8 The Adagio sostenuto as sonata form

As with the first movement of the E♭ Sonata, this movement's form is hard to categorise in the terms of any single textbook archetype. Most commentators have heard it either as a modified sonata form or as an irregular song form. While both models shed light on aspects of the movement, neither maps on to it with conviction. Sonata-form descriptions, such as Ilmari Krohn's (Figure 5.8), are at their most illuminating on the recapitulation (bars 42–60).[12] This section functions in a straightforwardly classical manner by remaining in the tonic and reprising the main ideas from the first part of the movement. But it is less convincing to interpret bars 1–41 as a sonata-form exposition and development.

Difficulties do not lie with taxonomic problems: identifying the 'second subject', or asking whether the development begins in the 'correct' key. Such questions forget that for classical composers sonata form was a flexible set of conventions, not a prescriptive form. Rather, a sonata-form description fails to convince here because the music seems to have little to do with even the most basic conventions of a sonata-form exposition. Seen against these conventions, bars 1–23 are in different ways both over-articulated in that perfect cadences in different keys regularly punctuate the music (in bars 5, 9, 15, and 23), and consequently no dynamic polarity is established between the tonic and relative major; and under-articulated in that the surface of the music is free of the gestural (and thematic) contrasts that punctuate the course of most expositions. In this movement there is little distinction between opening, middle, and closing ideas; in fact, all the phrases sound like permutations of one or two motives (see Example 5.6).

Peter Benary reflects this cyclical aspect in his analysis of the movement as a strophic song form (Figure 5.9).[13] He highlights its paratactic phrase groupings, its large-scale proportional symmetries (27:15:27 bars), and the framing function of its 'prelude', central section, and

bars	1–5	6–27	28–42		43–60	60–69
	Prelude	1st Strophe	Central section/pedal point		2nd Strophe	Coda

Figure 5.9 The Adagio sostenuto as song form

coda. Since he claims the movement as a prototypical Song Without Words, Benary's distinction between melodic and accompaniment sections is appropriate, but it cannot account for the vestigial aspects of sonata form mentioned above. For example, drawing parallels between the first and second strophes tends to play down both their different tonal functions and the important fact that the music gravitates towards the coda more strongly than towards the central section.

Alternatively the movement may be heard as a two-part form in which the first section modulates freely and the second prolongs the tonic. In this respect there is a striking similarity between the form of the Adagio sostenuto and the second movement ('Fantasia') of Haydn's String Quartet in E♭ Op. 76 no. 6 (see Figure 5.10).

In both cases the tonic is not brought into a sonata-like conflict with another key, but it forms the starting point for a wide-ranging modulation through several keys. Haydn's emphasis on mediant relations is the more capricious design; Beethoven's slow progress through a circle of fifths from E major and minor to the dominant of C♯ minor seems more inexorable. Like sonata form and song form, this two-part model cannot claim exclusively to hold the key to understanding the form of this movement. However, in comparison with the alternatives, it is relatively free of conceptual baggage. Consequently it is used as the basis for the following discussion.

Haydn

keys	B	c♯	E/e	G	B♭/b♭	B	A♭		B
bars	1	16	20	27	31	39	49		60–112

Beethoven

keys	c♯	E/e	b	f♯	c♯	G♯ (=V/c♯)		c♯
bars	1	9	15	23	27	28		42–69

Part 1: modulates freely	**Part 2: prolongs tonic**

Figure 5.10 Tonal designs of Haydn Op. 76/6/ii and Beethoven Op. 27/2/i

Introduction	bars 1–5³	(5 bars)	c♯
Phrase 1	5⁴–10³	(5)	c♯–E–e
Phrase 2	10⁴–15³	(5)	e – b
Phrase 3	15⁴–23	(8)	B (=V/e)–f♯
Phrase 4	23–8¹	(5)	f♯–V/c♯
V pedal	28–41	(14)	

Figure 5.11 Design of the Adagio sostenuto Part 1

One of the more remarkable qualities of 'Part 1' is the gap Beethoven opens between the formality of the topics and his informal treatment of them. The introduction and first two phrases all last for five bars (Figure 5.11). But the length and pacing of the melody within each phrase is varied so that the music evolves towards the eight-bar Phrase 3. There is also much harmonic variety. As Part 1 progresses the complexity and intensity of the harmony increases: bars 1–10 are diatonic; changes of mode colour Phrases 2 and 3 (E/e in bars 9–10, b/B in bar 15); chromatic passing chords are introduced (e.g. C as local ♭II in bar 12); and maximum intensity is reached in the exquisite dissonances of bars 16 and 18. Similarly, motives are developed in increasingly complex ways (Example 5.6). The melody's first phrase arises from the shape of the introduction. It contains three significant motives: an upper neighbour-note figure (x) interlocks with a stepwise descent through a fourth (y), and the close is signalled by a descending fifth (z). Example 5.6 is annotated to show subsequent reconfigurations of these shapes. In Phrase 2, x evolves into a turning figure around f♯¹ while y is implicit in the accompaniment at bars 13–15. Motive x continues to be transformed in Phrase 3: the dotted anacrusis disappears and the turning figure is chromaticised about c♯² (bars 15–17). Its extraordinary plaintive quality (an example of *Pathopoeia*) is underlined by its dissonant intervals with the bass. Chromaticism also infects y in this phrase: the descent through a fourth includes the 'Neapolitan' g♮¹ in bar 21. Phrase 4 breaks the pattern in several ways. It accelerates the harmonic unfolding to end with an imperfect cadence into V/c♯ in bars 27–8; it includes inversions of x and y; and it exceeds the melody's upper limit, moving above c♯² for the first time to reach e² at bar 27. It is tempting to interpret this climb to e² as a breakthrough, liberating the treble from the numbing constraints of the chant-derived melodies. But the treble immediately gravitates

Example 5.6 Motivic patterns in Part 1 of the Adagio sostenuto

back towards its 'natural' level, returning to b♯[1] in bar 28. A long pedal point on G♯ follows. Despite the inevitable accumulation of harmonic tension over this pedal, Beethoven suppresses much of the passage's dramatic potential by maintaining a quiet dynamic level and by creating an arch shape of the treble's register. Thus the section is not directed towards a climactic resolution, but reaches its climax at its midpoint in bar 35. Motive *x* is liquidated in bars 28–31 and the rest of the section is dominated by triplet broken chords. If the melody has previously kept the accompaniment in check, the triplets now become comparatively wild, spiralling through diminished seventh chords into a high register. But they sink back after bar 35, and echoes of bars 27–8 in bars 37–40 can only be interpreted as a profoundly pessimistic gesture, further intensified by the substitution of d♮ for d♯ in bar 39. All passion spent, the

Phrase 1	bars	42–6^3	(5 bars)	c#–E
Phrase 2		46^4–51^3	(5)	E–c#
Phrase 3		51^4–60^1	(8)	C#–c#
Coda		60–9	(10)	c#

Figure 5.12 Design of Adagio sostenuto Part 2

Example 5.7 Op. 27/2/i bars 47–54

bass outlines the turning figure based on x before cadencing into the tonic at bar 42.

Once C# minor has been recaptured it is never seriously threatened by other keys. Part 2 reprises most of the ideas from Part 1, but Beethoven compresses the themes and connects the phrases more strongly to one another. For example, an overarching pattern c#–E–c# links Phrases 1 and 2 (Figure 5.12), and Phrases 2 and 3 are run together and linked by motivic repetition (Example 5.7). Phrase 3 generates a climax: the descent from $c\#^2$ to $c\#^1$ (bars 55–60) is the movement's most mobile moment. It grows out of the 'plaintive cry', in response to the change to C# major in bar 51. This chord acts as V/f# (bar 55), initiating a series of perfect cadences (expressed as a descending 6–5 sequence). Such quickened harmonies are more than the movement can bear, and the next cadence into c# (bar 60) introduces a short coda. While the coda is primarily a peroration, winding down to the single C# in bar 68, it also has parallels with the central pedal point. Both sections do without a treble melody and allow the accompaniment's triplets to rise into a higher register. And both are based on a pedal G#, in the bass in the earlier section, tolling a funereal monotone in the tenor during the coda.

Beethoven does not activate the dramatic potential of his ideas in the Adagio sostenuto. Motives are not developed in a conversational or confrontational discourse, but are crafted into permutational combinations, looming in and out of focus over the uniform triplets. Thus each melodic phrase seems to offer a provisional arrangement of the ideas,

Allegretto	A¹ (varied repeat A²)	bars	0–16
	B		16–24
	A³		24–36
Trio	C		36–44
	D		44–60

Figure 5.13 Form of the Allegretto

rather than evolving towards the telos of a 'perfect' form. The coda is hardly a goal here, and the final bars are placed on a knife edge between closing and merely stopping. Rather than allowing the movement to drift from *pianissimo* into silence, Beethoven asks for the Allegretto to follow without a break.

Allegretto

This 'flower between two abysses'[14] brings yet another sudden shift in tone and character. Most critics have heard it as a necessary 'relief' from the strongly characterised outer movements, and it undoubtedly fills an important psychological space between the inactivity of the Adagio sostenuto and the finale's manic drama. Moreover its change of mode to the major (D♭ is an enharmonic spelling of C♯) provides a much needed perspective on the otherwise ubiquitous C♯ minor.[15]

Yet despite these surface contrasts there are numerous connections between the first two movements. Some are built into the pitch and rhythmic patterns, others are perhaps not inherent in the text but depend on choices made by performers. Bars 1–37 contain repeated descending fourths in the treble, thus developing the shape found in the bass at the opening of the Adagio. Section **B**, though superficially a contrast to the first sixteen bars, merely expands the all-pervasive motive (Example 5.8). Additionally the movement's characteristic rhythmic pattern (♩ | ♩♩ | ♩) can be perceived as a transformation of ♫ | ♩. ♫ | ♩. from the Adagio, though – as Tovey remarked – there is a new metrical ambiguity to this pattern in the Allegretto.[16] The music is organised in two-bar hypermetres, but it is not clear where the main accent should fall: ♩ | ♩♩♩♪♩ | ♩♪♩♩ or ♩♩♩ | ♩♪♩♩♪♩ | ♩? Some pianists underline the continuity of the sonata by maintaining a common pulse for the Adagio and the Allegretto (see p. 51 above). Others pursue the same goal by

85

Example 5.8 Motivic relationships in the Allegretto

moving from the first movement to the second with no intervening silence. In this way the first phrase of the Allegretto literally grows out of the Adagio's closing tonic, a feature which might explain why Beethoven takes so long to articulate the tonic chord strongly in section A^1 (bars 1–4 prolong V and the first root-position D♭ major chord comes only in bar 8).[17] But by the end of the A^3 the postponement of closure has become a more assertive idea as the bass circles round for an extra four bars before cadencing in bar 37. In comparison, the beginning of the Trio confidently projects the tonic with powerful root-position chords, but in other respects it seems to go over the same ground as the first section of the Allegretto. Both sections open with non-modulating phrases (bars 1–16 and 37–44); both have central phrases with descending chromatic lines (the treble in bars 17–24, the bass in bars 45–9); and in the last eight bars of the Trio (bars 53–60) the bass virtually quotes bars 32–6 from the earlier section. Thus the Allegretto may be seen to exhibit the same type of improvisatory variation processes that characterise sections of the E♭ fantasy-sonata.

This is the only movement in either of the Op. 27 sonatas which is not marked *attacca* to the next movement. Some pianists, however, plunge straight into the finale, following the spirit of Beethoven's score rather than its letter. The 'missing' *attacca* is unlikely to have been a mistaken omission: it is not in Beethoven's autograph and, had he intended to include the marking, he would surely have added it at the proof stage of the first edition. Paul Mies argued that an *attacca* would have been confusing within a *da capo* movement, and that its absence does not indicate a pause between the second and third movements.[18] Whatever the rights

Example 5.9 Registral connections between the Allegretto and Presto agitato

or wrongs of joining the finale to the Allegretto in performance, there are strong registral connections that override the double bar. Example 5.9 shows how a gap in the treble register at bars 34–6 is filled by ascending arpeggios in bars 1–2. So, if the Allegretto emerges in response to the last notes of the Adagio, then the finale appears to take its immediate cue from the gesture which precedes it.

Presto agitato

All the drama that was suppressed in the first movement bursts forth with a vengeance in the finale. Indeed the Presto agitato might almost be regarded as a recomposition of the Adagio sostenuto in Beethoven's most dramatic style. Aspects of the first movement's tonal design leave traces here (see the discussion of the development section, below). And earlier ideas return transformed within this, the most terse and concentrated sonata-form movement the composer had written up to this time. As several critics have pointed out, the opening section of the Presto dynamically recasts the beginning of the sonata: its arpeggios, *lament* bass, and emphasis on G♯. But the other themes also refer back to the previous movements (see Example 5.10). For instance, the second subject inverts the Adagio sostenuto's basic melodic shape (5.10a and b); the theme at bars 43ff. alludes to the head-motive of the Allegretto (5.10c and d); the end of the development section recalls the end of the Adagio's central pedal point (5.10e and f); the coda returns to the first movement's triplet quavers and slow sonorous bass lines; and in both the first and last movements Neapolitan chords are prominent. In comparison with the looser motivic connections and mixed character of the E♭ Sonata, the 'Moonlight' has a remarkable motivic cohesion and – in its outer movements —unity of tone.

Example 5.10 Motivic transformations in the Presto agitato

	Bars	Tonality	Length
Exposition	1–64	c♯–g♯	64 bars
Development	65–101	(C♯)–f♯–G–f♯–V/c♯	37 bars
Recapitulation	102–57	c♯	56 bars
Coda	157–200	c♯	43 bars

Figure 5.14 form of the Presto agitato

Figure 5.14 gives an overview of the movement's form. The opening of the exposition is built on two broad descents from C♯ to G♯[1] in the bass: the first (bars 1–14) moves by step and ends with a six-bar prolongation of G♯ as the dominant of C♯; in the second (bars 15–21) the bass arpeggiates through C♯, A♯, and F𝄪, before resolving onto G♯ as a new tonic in bar 21. The following theme pays lip service to the lyrical archetype for second subjects, but it retains the nervous energy of the opening with its rapid Alberti bass, gruppetto, and sudden dynamic surges. A perfect cadence in G♯ minor might be expected at bar 29, but Beethoven substitutes a third-inversion dominant seventh chord. This substitution initiates a descending sequence (bars 29–32) that transforms elements of the Adagio sostenuto: the melodic shape of the 'plaintive cry' in bars 15–17 and the sweeping harmonic pattern of bars 56–7. It is halted only by a thunderous A major chord in bar 33, the strongest emphasis yet on a Neapolitan chord. An attempt at closure is thwarted by another inter-rupted cadence at bar 37, and the first strong close in G♯ minor finally arrives at bar 43. In contrast to the second subject, the closing theme is harmonically stable, dissipating earlier dissonant energies with a series of cadential formulae. The exposition's last cadence is coloured by another Neapolitan (A major in bar 55), before the second subject is liq-uidated over a G♯ pedal (bars 57–64). At the close a repeated emphasis on $\hat{5}$ (d♯³) recalls both the finale's second subject and the monotone that dominated the Adagio sostenuto. In bars 63–5 chromatic motion in an inner voice (b–b♯–c♯¹) retonicises C♯ minor for the exposition repeat. At the second-time bar the music cadences into C♯ major rather than C♯ minor: a modification which leads to F♯ minor at the start of the develop-ment.

At thirty-seven bars, the development section (bars 65–101) is unusu-ally short and concentrated. It is governed by two tonal areas: F♯ minor acts as a local tonic until bar 83, at which point the music swings rapidly towards the dominant of C♯ in preparation for the recapitulation. This progression transforms a weak relationship from the first movement into a dynamic, goal-directed process here. In Part 1 of the Adagio sostenuto the last perfect cadence is in F♯ minor (bar 23), initiating a move to the dominant of C♯ (bars 23–8) and a long pedal point. The Presto's develop-ment section dramatises this progression, but a significant new element is incorporated: the G major statement of the second subject (bar 79 onwards) is a Neapolitan interpolation within the ruling F♯ minor, further developing the increasingly important relationships between key areas a semitone apart (for a tonal outline of this section, see Example 5.11).

Beethoven tightens the drama of the recapitulation by omitting the modulatory passage from the exposition: the second subject, now in

Example 5.11 Op. 27/2/iii Harmonic outline of the development section

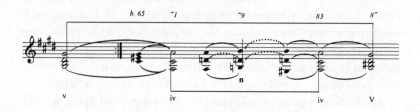

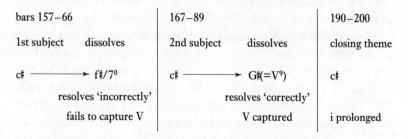

bars 157–66		167–89		190–200
1st subject	dissolves	2nd subject	dissolves	closing theme
c♯ ⟶ f♯/7⁰		c♯ ⟶ G♯(=V⁹)		c♯
resolves 'incorrectly'		resolves 'correctly'		
fails to capture V		V captured		i prolonged

Figure 5.15 Form of the Coda in Op. 27/2/iii

the tonic, directly follows the fermata on G♯ in bar 115. The rest of the recapitulation closely mirrors the closing sections of the exposition, and attention is shifted towards a long, elaborate coda. As in the E♭ Sonata, the coda reintroduces the topic of musical spontaneity. Thematically it covers the same ground as the recapitulation (see Figure 5.15), but ideas are compressed even further. The result of this compression, however, is that its different components are more loosely connected than before: the themes keep breaking down into cadenza-like flourishes. Moreover, dissonant chords fail to resolve properly (as in bar 166), there are changes of tempo (bars 187–90), and reminiscences of the opening Adagio sostentuto become increasingly obvious.

The coda begins with a restatement of the opening theme over yet another descending bass progression from C♯ (bar 157 onwards). But the bass overshoots the dominant in bar 163, and the theme disintegrates into swirling diminished seventh chords on F𝄪 (bars 163–4) and F♯ (bars 165–6). Startling discontinuities follow. The diminished seventh on F♯ resolves 'incorrectly' on to a root-position tonic chord in a different register, the dynamic suddenly drops to *piano*, and the second subject appears in the bass, just as in the development section. As the second subject gathers momentum it reprises the coda's initial descending bass progression (bars 175–7), and, like the first subject, it dissolves into improvisatory arpeggios whose triplet rhythms clearly recall the first movement. In bar 179 the Neapolitan chord makes a last emphatic appearance before the bass rises chromatically through F_x (supporting a diminished seventh in bars 181–2) to a second-inversion tonic chord at bar 183. As in the first sonata, the 'cadenza' ends on a V^9 followed by an unbarred *Eingang* (bar 187), a moment of poetic introspection amidst the headlong rush for closure. Two motionless Adagio bars finally lead to a tonic resolution at bar 190. The following reprise and disintegration of the closing theme provides an ultimate point of contact with the first movement: the monotone G♯ is emphasised once again; the suppressed wildness of the Adagio's arpeggios is unfettered in bars 196–8; even the last three chords can be seen as a transformation of the end of the first movement, resigned pessimism giving way to defiance.

6

The design of the Op. 31 sonatas

Beethoven distanced the Op. 27 sonatas from eighteenth-century precedents by amalgamating the sonata with the fantasy, but in Op. 31 he strikes a more searching attitude towards fundamental aspects of classical syntax and the sonata style. In some respects the design of Op. 31 is more conventional than that of Op. 27: movements are discreet and closed; each sonata begins with a fast movement in sonata form; and – with the exception of the third sonata – the distribution of movement types has ample precedent in the classical repertoire. However, the relationship between form and content, especially in the first movements of Op. 31, is even more innovative and fantastic than in Op. 27. Several common threads run through Op. 31. Each sonata begins with an unstable opening, whose implications profoundly affect the subsequent discourse. And multi-movement integration becomes increasingly important in each successive sonata: from gestural rhymes and a certain degree of complementarity between the outer movements of the first sonata, to a more thoroughly processual integration between the outer movements of the last.

No. 1 in G

Allegro vivace

One of the most innovative aspects of the first group (bars 1–64) is the way in which Beethoven seems to revel in a lack of eloquence. Gestures are disjointed and phrases asymmetrical. By turn highly volatile and circular, the music repeatedly returns to its starting point before striking out in new directions. Yet there is an underlying pattern which gives the opening section coherence. While Beethoven completely eschews

Example 6.1 Op. 31/1/i bars 1–8

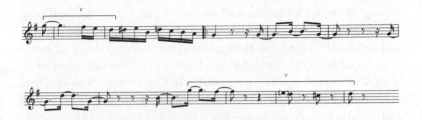

Example 6.2 Op. 31/1/i Chromatic expansion of the head-motive

conventional antecedent-consequent structures, each phrase is connected to its neighbours by a clear chain of causes and effects; moreover, short initiating gestures tend to provoke longer responses. For example, in the first phrase a three-bar run is answered by an eight-bar segment. A descending octave (g^2–g^1) in bars 1–3 is met by an ascending octave (g^1–g^2) arpeggiated over bars 3–8. The lack of co-ordination between the hands at the very start is taken up in bars 4–9: synchronisation is achieved only at the final cadence in bar 10. And the end of the phrase contains a hidden repetition of the head-motive (marked 'v' in Example 6.1).

Similarly, the entire eleven-bar phrase provokes a more highly developed (and harmonically mobile) response in bars 12–30. The sudden appearance of F major (♭VII) at bar 11 has prompted much critical comment. It has commonly been compared to the descending pattern at the start of the 'Waldstein' Sonata Op. 53 (1804). As Example 6.2 shows, F major is part of a descending pattern which might be interpreted as a chromaticised expansion of the movement's head-motive. While the descending tetrachord is hardly novel in itself, its innovation springs from the unprecedentedly dramatic way with which Beethoven unfolds it. As Hugo Riemann pointed out, a circle of fifths underpins bars 11–26 (F–C–G–V/G), and the repeated G major cadences in bars 25–30 form an emphatic response to the D major cadence at bars 10–11.[1]

The recapture of G major is celebrated by a brilliant-style elaboration of the movement's head-motive in bars 30–45. This is the most fluent passage so far, yet for all its sound and fury it only succeeds in outlining an imperfect cadence. The hyperbole of its climactic rhetoric is comically pricked by a reprise of the opening at bar 46. When the much anticipated modulation to a secondary key finally occurs, it is unconventional, abrupt, and a model of motivic economy. In bars 53–4 an F♯ major chord substitutes for D major, audaciously preparing the tonicisation of B (III). And in bars 55–65 the new key is grounded by repeated incises that rhythmically augment a chromatic quirk from bar 2.

Beethoven's unusual choice of key for the second group has provoked much comment. Both Marx and Tovey view the use of B major/minor not as the product of Beethoven's *Willkür*, but as a logical step provoked by elements from the first group. For Marx, the over-emphatic V chords in bars 39–45 demand an alternative to V for the subsidiary theme.[2] But Tovey conversely attributed the substitution of V by III to the dominant's relative *weakness* in the face of the strong use of IV and ♭VII in the first group: 'such bold treatment of the nearer keys makes the dominant ineffective as a key for a contrasted section'.[3] The choice of B (as opposed to other alternatives to D) might have been suggested by the fact that it is the third note of the G major triad, forming what Schenkerian theorists term a 'third divider'; the B minor triad shares two notes with G major (hence the laconic retransition at the end of the exposition); and two pitches that receive a very strong melodic emphasis in the second group are D♯ and D♮, echoing the chromatic quirk (d^2–$d\sharp^2$) from bar 2.

The second group evolves as a complex chain of statements, variations, and extensions (see Figure 6.1). It begins with an eight-bar contredanse theme, divided into complementary antecedent-consequent phrases, whose rhythmic fluency and major mode were surely designed to form a maximum contrast with the first group. At bar 74 the theme migrates to the bass, where it appears in the minor and in *Sturm und Drang* style. Its antecedent phrase is followed by a more mobile, extended continuation that rises to an apex on a in bars 82–3 before falling sequentially back to B. At bar 88 the treble begins a variation of the extension, cadencing at bar 98. The remaining bars of the exposition liquidate the treble pattern from bars 96^2–98^1, before a *forte* g^2 (bar 111) wrenches the music back to G for the exposition repeat.

Bars	Phrase lengths	Idea			Voice	Key
66–73	4+4	x^1	x^2		treble	B
74–88	4+10	x^1		y	bass	b
88–98	10			y	treble	b
98–112	10+4					b (liquidation)

Figure 6.1 Allegro vivace exposition second group

At the start of the development Beethoven plays with ambiguities created by the interaction of goal-oriented and circular elements in his design. As at the exposition repeat (which must be taken, if the movement is to make sense), G major returns, thus launching the development in the tonic. An obvious pitfall of this strategy is that the premature return of I might lower the harmonic tension accumulated in the exposition, thereby undercutting the development's harmonic role. But Beethoven side-steps this danger. In the short term G only functions as the local tonic momentarily: by bar 119 its function has become V/c. More ingeniously, the innovative design of the exposition also allows Beethoven to avoid a structural *faux pas*. Since the expository second group tonicises III instead of the usual V, the function of this particular development section is to *progress* to V, not to prolong it. The return of G major at the beginning of the development is thus merely a staging post in the progression from III to V, rather than a structural return of the tonic.

The development moves through two harmonic cycles: a flatward circle of fifths takes the music from G to B♭ in bars 112–34, and a step-wise ascent leads from B♭ through C minor to D minor in bars 134–50. Once D has been achieved Beethoven converts it into V/g by reintroducing F♯, and the section ends with a massive prolongation of V from bar 158 to bar 193. The length of the closing pedal point was doubtless precipitated by two factors from the exposition: by the need first to cap the emphatic V pedal from bars 39–45, and second to compensate for the tonicisation of III in the second group. Additionally, Beethoven required sufficient space to effect a convincing transition from the development's brilliant-style passagework to the more fragmented rhythmic groups of the opening theme: hence the introduction of the stuttering motive as an ostinato at bar 170, and its subsequent liquidation.

Beethoven's innovative design for the exposition and his pacing of the

Bars	Phrase lengths	Idea			Voice	Key
218–25	4+4	x^1	x^2		treble	E
226–33	4+4	x^1		x^3	bass	e → V/G
234–41	4+4	x^1	x^2		treble	G
242–56	4+10	x^1		y	bass	G
256–66	10			y	treble	G
266–80	10+4					G (liquidation)

Figure 6.2 Allegro vivace recapitulation: second group

development section have profound consequences for the recapitulation. He reworks, rather than reprises, the contents of the exposition. The first group is abridged. No doubt the brilliant passagework from bars 30–45 is cut because its strong V emphasis would be redundant in the wake of the development's closing V pedal. Therefore the progression through F major and C major that led to the exposition's V pedal is cut also. Instead, in bars 194–216 Beethoven conflates aspects of bars 1–11 and 46–64, taking the music unconventionally to E major for the second group of themes in bar 218. Since a basic premise of classical sonata form is the demand for tonal resolution, Beethoven expands the second group to effect a modulation back to G major (Figure 6.2: compare with Figure 6.1, illustrating the parallel section of the exposition, above).

This strategy has precedents in the first movements of the two earlier C minor Sonatas, Op. 10 no. 1 and Op. 13, in which the second subject is recapitulated in the 'wrong' key (F minor on both occasions) before modulating back to the tonic. But it acquires a new power in Op. 31 no. 1 because while E major is structurally the 'wrong' key, it is – paradoxically – 'right' in view of the exposition's unusual tonal design.

The brilliant passagework expunged from the recapitulation's first group is reprised at the start of the coda in bar 280, ending once again on an unresolved V (bar 295). In the exposition the dominant resolved to the tonic immediately at bar 46; but in the coda Beethoven sustains V for six bars beyond the fermata, a bizarre gesture which evidently puzzled Nägeli. One merely has to play the passage with Nägeli's inserted bars to see what a masterpiece of comic timing Beethoven's original is. The lack of a tonic answer to the dominant at bars 196–8 provides exactly the right amount of asymmetry and instability to maintain a sense of momentum through the final six perfect cadences. At last, the harmonic restlessness that has gone hand in hand with the music's gestural instability gives way to relative repose.

Adagio grazioso

Admirers of the more self-consciously serious slow movements in Beethoven's early sonatas have never quite been able to disguise their disappointment at the relative frivolity of the Adagio grazioso. Beethoven's appropriation of a popular salon style, his evocation of song with guitar accompaniment, a main theme suspiciously similar to a famous melody by Haydn, and the simplicity of the movement's form – all have been cited with derogatory implications. Yet in the context of Nägeli's commission, Beethoven's strategy makes much sense. If the Adagio grazioso might have been aimed primarily at those who were yet to be converted to Beethoven's idiosyncratic style, then in contrast the D minor Sonata's Adagio targeted connoisseurs of the composer's music, while the third sonata radically dispensed with a slow movement altogether. In the Adagio grazioso Beethoven competes with Hummel and Dussek (two composers whose works were also featured in Nägeli's *Répertoire*) on their home ground. Moreover, it is a very superior example of its type, with formal subtleties and a range of tone that have not always received their critical due. For instance, serenade-like prettiness is largely confined to the opening theme, and is starkly contrasted with pathos and high sentiment elsewhere in the movement. Similarly, some formal analyses have played down whole layers of ambiguity. Tovey described the movement as a ternary form with coda (Figure 6.3).[4]

A	bars 1–26	(26)
B	27–64	(38)
A	65–90	(26)
Coda	91–119	(29)

Figure 6.3 Tovey's formal analysis of the Adagio grazioso

A	B	bars 1–64	Antecedent (Major minor; open-ended)
A	Coda	bars 65–119	Consequent (Major major; closed)

Figure 6.4 Implicit two-part form of the Adagio grazioso

While it cannot be denied that the movement unfolds against the background of ternary form, several aspects of the music supplement and even run counter to this interpretation. Most obviously, there is a rondo element: each of the four sections begins with an eight-bar refrain. And cutting across the ternary design is an implicit two-part form (antecedent-consequent) as shown in Figure 6.4.

Within each section there is a greater mobility than might be expected in a lyrical piece. Take the first section (bars 1–26). The refrain (bars 1–8) is essentially a closed thematic statement, cadencing into C at bar 8; but its melody contains an asymmetry that is sufficient to generate a long movement, not just an eight-bar miniature. As the treble pirouettes its way through an ascending scale from c^2 (bar 1), it overshoots a triadically consonant goal (g^2, bar 5), reaching its apex instead on the dissonant a^2 in bar 6. Both the pitch A and the sixth degree of the scale assume an increasingly important motivic function as the movement progresses. It falls to the answering phrase (bars 9–16) to realise the refrain's implicit mobility (Example 6.3). In bar 9 the refrain's headmotive is transferred to the bass, climbing from C to D in the next four bars. At bar 13 the treble takes over the next melodic pitch, E, but treats it as $\hat{6}/G$, rather than as $\hat{3}/C$. Thus the next four bars see a melodic descent to g^1, accompanied by a perfect cadence in G. Yet even this cadence does not signify unambiguous closure in a new key. Is one perfect cadence enough to tonicise G? In truth, the cadence at bar 16 lies in a grey area, in which G functions somewhere between a strongly prepared dominant and a very weakly prepared tonic.

On this note of uncertainty a startling change of tone occurs. Control, polish, urbanity vanish; delicate ornaments drop away, leaving an alien, dissonant music which is more raw, perplexing, and immediate than the refrain. The new phrase is expressively alien, but its melodic motives are clearly derived from bars 5–6 (the rising fourth e^2–a^2 is transposed to $c\sharp^2$–f^2 in bars 18–19, and to b^1–e^2 in bars 21–2). Similarly, many of the obfuscatory chromatic details – such as the $e\flat^1$ in bar 17, and the minor

Example 6.3 Op. 31/1/ii Motivic basis of bars 1–16

ninth chord in bar 18 – disguise a straightforward progression: two perfect cadences (in D minor at bars 18–19, and C at bars 21–2) and an imperfect cadence to V/C (bars 22–3). But in terms of their expressive weight they are far more significant than the opulent details of the refrain. Beethoven's juxtaposition of cultured and raw sentiment here inevitably brings to mind the topical antitheses of Op. 27 no. 1. And, as in the first two movements of the fantasy sonata, the 'cultured' topics overcome the 'uncultured' with a short *Eingang* on the dominant at bar 26.

When the opening theme returns, lightly decorated in the treble, at bar 27, most of its new figuration is purely ornamental. But the semi-quaver scale ascending to f^3 in bar 33 proves to have a more enduring thematic significance, giving rise to one of the main ideas in the next section. In bar 34 the theme cadences in C major, but the music turns immediately to the minor. *Minore* sections in classical rondo and ternary forms conventionally allowed some freedom of modulation, but here Beethoven remarkably begins to establish A♭ major as a subsidiary tonic in bar 36, after just one bar of C minor. At first the noble simplicity of the new treble melody at bar 36 brings a sharp contrast of tone with the first section; but the high sentimental style is abandoned at bar 41, and replaced by a series of exchanges between treble and bass, built on a retrograde of the treble at bar 33. The exchanges modulate from A♭ to F minor in bars 41–8, before a faster chain of sixths descends to C minor in bars 49–51. Finally, an imperfect cadence leads to a massive twelve-bar prolongation of the dominant of C. No doubt the astonishing length of the pedal point was prompted by several factors: it balances the preceding twelve bars of staccato semiquaver figuration; it accumulates harmonic tension more effectively than any earlier section of the movement, thus giving greater weight to its resolution at the subsequent reprise of the refrain; and it gives Beethoven the scope to accomplish an ascending registral shift from the bass-heavy sonorities of the *Minore* section to the lighter serenade style of the refrain.

An ornamented reprise of the entire first section follows, culminating in a more ambitious *Eingang* at bar 90. The final section begins in bar 91 with the most luxuriantly decorated version of the refrain. But at bar 99 Beethoven changes the established pattern: instead of answering the treble with a bass statement of the theme, a succession of two new paragraphs follows. At first there is a gradual foreshortening of phrase lengths: from eight bars (refrain melody) to 5+5 (bars 99–108; the last bar elided with the first of the next phrase), then 2+2 and 1+1. But the process is relaxed at the peroration in bars 114–19, where the bars are grouped 2+1. At the same time that the phrases are compressed, various elements of the refrain are abstracted and arranged into new configurations. In bars 99–101, for example, the predominance of trills can be traced back obviously to the refrain's head-motive, whereas the climactic emphasis on the subdominant (bars 100^3–101^2) transfigures the melodic apex of the opening theme (a^2). Conversely, the circle-of-fifths progression in bars 99–100 has no obvious antecedent in this movement, but the descending chromatic line in the alto (c^1–b–b♭–a) is a clear throwback to the chromatic progression underpinning the opening movement's first paragraph. From bar 108 Beethoven liquidates elements of the head-motive. For the first time in the coda, the *Minore* section casts its shadow, with repeated A♭–G figures in the bass (bars 111–13), answered by a chromatic ascent to the tonic in bars 114–15. Other aspects of the central section continue to exert an influence at the movement's end. Although the melodic resolution at bar 115 would appear to have the last word, Beethoven repeats it with increasing intensity in the following three bars, each time a third higher. Thus there is a final reminiscence of the refrain's melodic descent from A in bars 117–18: a figure which concurrently harks back to the end of the *Minore* section (cf. bars 62^3–64). Similarly, the sonorous, bass-heavy textures of bars 114–18 recall the *Minore*'s brief moments of high sentimentality. But finally, with the utmost delicacy, Beethoven restores the serenade-like quality with a final cadence in the highest possible octave.

Rondo: Allegretto

The lyrical mode of the Adagio is maintained to an unusual degree in the Finale, a sonata rondo with distinctly conservative tendencies. Mozart's late keyboard music – especially the first movement of his Sonata in F K. 533 (1788) and the Finale of his Sonata in D K. 576 (1789) – is called to mind by this movement's two- and three-part contrapuntal writing, its use of textural inversion, its delicate triplet figurations, and by the short cadenza that breaks out just before the final stretto.

The opening refrain is built from two statements – first in the treble, then in the bass – of a two-part theme in the gavotte style. Its formal symmetry is mirrored at a more detailed level: the first part of the theme consists of four-bar antecedent and consequent phrases, and the second part of a repeated four-bar phrase. Such placid regularity forms an obvious foil to the nervous asymmetries of the first movement's opening theme. Similarly the refrain's harmonic stasis also contrasts with the highly mobile progressions of the first movement's opening paragraphs, and the harmonic outline of the refrain (V–I) reverses the I–V outline of bars 1–45 in the Allegro. Only at bar 32 of the Finale, where the last incise of the bass theme is answered in E minor by the treble, is tonal dynamism injected into the discourse. This statement and answer pattern between the bass and treble culminates in repeated perfect cadences on to A (V/V) in bars 35–42, as if in preparation for a second subject. However, the rest of the exposition is not conventionally thematic, but is dominated instead by brilliant triplet figuration. Bars 42–52 ground the new tonic (D) with increasingly emphatic cadences, decorated by triplet quaver figures derived from bar 17. A closing theme begins conventionally enough in bar 52 with rising broken chords in the treble. But at bar 60 the introduction of c♮^{1} in the tenor swings the music back towards G and a tonic reprise of the refrain begins in bar 66. Taking a leaf out of Mozart's book, Beethoven continues the closing theme's triplet figuration through into the reprise, so that the sectional nature of rondo form is somewhat disguised by the textural continuity.

The central developmental episode begins at bar 82 with a minor-mode version of the refrain in the bass. This flowers into a three-part fugato at bar 86: first with a quasi-canon between the bass and tenor, followed by a treble entry in C minor at bar 90, and a further canon between

Example 6.4 Op. 31/1/iii Harmonic outline of the development section

the treble and bass, leading to a cadence in E♭ major at bar 98. From this point the topic changes every four bars or so, brilliant-style triplet figuration alternating with repeated statements of the refrain's head-motive. The music modulates rapidly, from E♭ to C minor in bars 102–6, then through a circle of fifths, touching on F minor (bar 114) and B♭ minor (bar 117), finally descending by step from B♭ minor to G minor in bars 117–21. The final part of the episode contains three large-scale imperfect cadences in G minor (bars 121–5, 125–7, and 127–9), preparing a final return of the refrain. In comparison with the single-minded processes found in other development sections of Op. 31, the indirect route taken by this episode seems haphazard. Nevertheless, its frequent changes of topic and texture hide a characteristic overarching progression – which inverts the movement's turning head-motive (Example 6.4).

When the refrain reappears in bar 132 Beethoven once again uses an idea from the close of the previous episode as the basis for textural variation. Here the octave Ds remain invariant in the middle of the texture, and their triplet rhythms infect large areas of the opening theme. Aside from the textural variation of the refrain, however, the recapitulation largely mirrors the exposition. Uncharacteristically, Beethoven does not dramatise his harmonic modifications to the transition section: extra bars touching on the subdominant and supertonic minor are inserted unobtrusively at bars 166–70. From bar 196 the recapitulation's closing theme is modified: instead of leading to C major (in parallel with the exposition), a chromatic progression in an inner voice (b–c^1–$c\sharp^1$–d^1 in bars 196–200) leads to a second-inversion tonic chord. For six bars this chord is decorated in the bass with augmentations of the head-motive (E–D–C♯–D), culminating with a caesura in bar 206. An abrupt change of topic at bar 206, the brilliant style giving way to invertible counter-point over a pedal, marks the beginning of a cadenza in the fantasy style. At its heart lies a transformation of the movement's opening eight bars into a hymn-like cantabile (bars 224–42). But before the theme has cadenced properly it is succeeded by a Presto in the comic style, domi-nated by the over-emphatic repetition of the turning head-motive, with multiple cadences hammering home closure. In the last eight bars the coda echoes the end of the first movement, a gestural rhyme which pays lip service to multi-movement integration rather than foregrounding a concept that has been fundamental to the sonata as a whole.

As a design, this cadenza-Presto succession is reminiscent of the end of the E♭ Sonata in Op. 27. But there are telling differences between the two. In the coda of the E♭ Sonata expressive and comic elements are bal-anced on a knife edge, but here the comic is clearly paramount. The *Empfindsamerstil* transformation of the opening theme in bars 224–42 sounds forced: its segmentation into separate incises, alternating Alle-gretto and Adagio, seems like a clumsy attempt to achieve the type of effortless sensibility of the E♭ Sonata's Larghetto. Ultimately, this is mock-seriousness, not the genuine article, and its build-up of comic potential is discharged in the Presto.

No. 2 in D minor ('The Tempest')

Expressively enigmatic and shot through with formal ambiguities, the first movement of the D minor Sonata has continued to intrigue critics and performers to a greater extent than any of Beethoven's earlier sonata movements. Whatever reservations might be held about the work's connection with Shakespeare's play, the first movement is undeniably tempestuous. Owen Jander has even shown how Beethoven transfigures many imitative techniques from popular late-eighteenth-century storm music.[5] But if many of the individual gestures have mimetic origins, most twentieth-century critics have preferred to view them as transcendental. Moreover, it hardly does justice to the movement's rich and strange expressive qualities to focus exclusively on its stormi-ness. Lawrence Kramer has explored fractures in the first movement's expressive domain. In contrast to the prevalent *Sturm und Drang* in the Allegro sections, there are islands of pathetic sensibility at nodal points in the formal unfolding of the movement: the openings of the exposition, development, and recapitulation. While the *Sturm und Drang* Allegros invoke the sublime, inducing fear, terror and confusion, the Largo-Adagio passages (which Kramer terms 'sympathetic reserves') rouse feelings of pity, compassion and sympathy. Many structuralist critics have played down these contrasts, pointing to motivic and contrapuntal connections with the Allegro sections. But Kramer emphasises their lack of integration: for him, these moments are *parergon* ('outside the work'), serving to highlight what is missing from the primarily tempestuous discourse, human sympathy. Drawing a parallel with ideas current in late-eighteenth-century speculative anthropology, Kramer hears Beethoven trying to forge a new kind of subjectivity in this movement, not one based on 'the edifying perception of a musical object, but on the listening subject's sympathetic capacity to recognise another subject'.[6]

The movement's formal ambiguities have also generated much discussion. While Tovey felt that the application of conventional terminology would 'do no harm', most later writers have been more circumspect. The taxonomic difficulties encountered by most writers (for example, where does the introduction end and the first theme begin?) have arisen from two contrasting concepts of form: conformational (in which pre-existing models largely guide the course of the music), and generative (in which the shape of the music springs directly from its unique components). Of course, far from being mutually exclusive, these two concepts are symbiotic. Any piece is a unique expression of the formal principles it embodies, by virtue of its unique components. On the other hand, it makes no sense to hear music from the early nineteenth century – however original it might be – without recourse to a conformational formal background, in this case sonata form.

Yet the most influential formal accounts of the first movement have displayed a distinct bias towards the generative. Carl Dahlhaus stressed that 'the contradiction between motivicism, syntax, and harmony' here should be understood 'as the vehicle for a dialectics, by means of which *the form of the movement comes into being as a musically perceived transformation process*'.[7] For Dahlhaus, Beethoven's 'new path' of 1802 was virtually synonymous with the composer's novel concept of form-as-process, a quality best exemplified in the first movement of the 'Tempest' Sonata. In Dahlhaus's reading of the movement, the perception of form-as-process is invited by the contradictions between motivic development and formal function in bars 1–21 and bars 21–41. Essentially, he argues that bars 1–21 are constructed like an introduction but function as a first theme, while the passage beginning at bar 21 has the characteristics of a theme but functions as a transition. Ultimately, conformational terms like 'first theme' and 'transition' have a very limited application here; instead, the generative aspect of the exposition, whose music embodies a processual evolution, is highlighted. Janet Schmalfeldt – in a critique of Dahlhaus's analysis – subscribes to his dialectical system, but places a significantly different emphasis on the relationships between motives and ambiguous formal functions.[8] Schmalfeldt argues that in bars 1–21 introduction *becomes* theme: fantasy characteristics (such as motivic discontinuity, tempo variation, and an absence of clearly articulated harmonic goals) imperceptibly give way to 'thematic' properties like motivic continuity, tempo stability, and harmonic goal-orientation. Similarly, in bars 21–41 theme becomes transition, transformed from a state of harmonic stability (i–V–i in bars 21–30) to the type of instability that facilitates a modulation to the dominant. In a close reading of the entire exposition, Schmalfeldt proposes that the music constantly invites re-assessment of formal functions. Since these functions are constantly evolving, the music can be perceived in the process of becoming. While an elaboration of Schmafeldt's dialectical model to cover the whole movement is beyond the scope of this handbook, it is necessary briefly to outline some of the technical means by which the composer accomplishes his radical formal experiment, and their consequences in the development and recapitulation.

(1) Beethoven employs a peculiar type of motivic development. The flexibility with which he habitually developed motives has been noted and praised from his day to ours, but in this movement it is the inflexible deployment of three basic motives that is most striking. The opening arpeggio retains its features so consistently that it would be invidious to list its later appearances. Two-note groups from the start of the subsequent Allegro reappear only in bars 41–54 and the parallel passage in the recapitulation, while the treble descent a^1–d^1 ($\hat{5}$–$\hat{1}$) in bars 2–3 returns in a simplified form to dominate the end of the exposition and

Example 6.5 Op. 31/2/i Chromatic turn motives

recapitulation (e.g., e^3–a^2 in bars 70–5). Most spectacularly, the chromatic turn around a^1 which first emerges in bars 5–6 returns at bar 22 and at bar 55 with its pitches intact (Example 6.5). What counts for motivic development in this movement, then, is not changes to the motives themselves, but the new formal functions they acquire as the music plays out its process of becoming. Hence Beethoven's treatment of motives places the strongest possible emphasis on the processual quality of the music. In keeping with this principle, the development section is unusually brief, and uncharacteristically contains no more fragmentation and liquidation of motives than the exposition. Following the sudden tonicisation of F♯ minor in bar 99, attention is firmly focused on the simple contrapuntal process that leads the music back to V/i by bar 121.

(2) Beethoven achieves the sense of an unstoppable transformation process by constructing the music in unprecedentedly long spans, avoiding strong cadential closure. This technique is set up by the off-tonic opening. Although the dominant resolves immediately to a tonic chord at bar 3, in rhetorical terms the resolution is fatally weakened by the dominant caesura at the end of the phrase (bar 6). Thus the first strong arrival in the tonic appears only in bar 21. Conventional expectations would suggest that the tonicisation of A in the second part of the exposition should be grounded with a strong arrival in A minor. But Beethoven postpones an emphatic close until the last possible moment (bar 87). Earlier he uses every technique at his disposal to postpone closure. When the V/V pedal (bars 41–54) finally resolves to A minor, it is to a relatively

unstable first inversion (bar 55), weakened further by the Neapolitan chord at the end of the bar. Similarly, closure is weakened at bar 63 by the elision of two phrases and another Neapolitan disruption; at bar 69 by an interrupted cadence; at bars 75, 79 and 83 by the bass E pedal; at bars 77 and 81 by the beginning of a treble descent from $\hat{5}$ (e^3); and at bar 85 by the avoidance of melodic closure, since the treble has fallen to $\hat{3}$, not $\hat{1}$. Hence there is a singular lack of cadential articulation in the exposition.

The postponement of closure is intensified in the development and recapitulation. Paradoxically, the appearance of the tonic major at the start of the development (bar 93) raises, rather than lowers, the harmonic tension: it does not function locally as a stable tonic, but as the first step on a mysterious harmonic journey that unfolds in the subsequent Largo bars. Although the move from A minor to F♯ minor in bars 88–99 can be pinned down to a series of chromatic transformations, Beethoven surely designed this elliptical passage to produce an increasingly disorienting effect on listeners. He omits chords that would have made this section syntactically 'normal', so that even the F♯ minor that launches the next Allegro emerges from a change of mode, rather than from a perfect cadence.

If the avoidance of perfect cadences thus colours the start of the development, it has more far-reaching consequences for its end. The proportionately long V preparation in bars 121–38 carries obvious implications for a strong confirmatory arrival in D minor at the start of the recapitulation. But, however obvious, these implications are not realised. The recapitulation begins with recitative-like expansions of the opening Largo bars' pauses. As at the start of the movement, resolutions into D minor are very weak (and in bar 148 only implied), having a purely local significance that is overridden by the caesura on A at bar 152. The second recitative (bars 155–8), in F minor, makes the possibility of strong tonic resolution even more remote. As if the music has worked itself into a dead end, it is followed by a 'new' Allegro passage (bars 159–70) which modulates – via an enharmonic switch to F♯ minor – back to V/d. If, in Schmalfeldt's terms, 'introduction becomes theme' in the exposition, in the recapitulation introduction becomes transition. In short, this section refuses to behave in a conformational recapitulatory manner. It marks a return to the opening idea, but in an altered state that obfuscates rather than clarifies. And it resolves none of the harmonic tension accumulated in the exposition and development. From the 1780s Haydn and Mozart occasionally played with the postponement of tonic return at the start of their recapitulations. In this movement Beethoven pushes the technique to its extreme. A significant effect of the new passage at bars 159–70 is that the strong tonic arrival in bar 21 is not reca-pitulated. Although the music is clearly in D minor from at least bar 171, the first strong arrival on the tonic occurs only twelve bars before the end of the movement, at bar 217. This bar is thus simultaneously the moment of structural closure and, remarkably, the only strong D minor cadence other than at bar 21. This is surely the goal to which the form-as-process has been aimed, and nothing is left for the coda (bars 219–28) except to add weight to the final tonic with ten bars of unadulterated D minor.

Nothing is left for the coda to accomplish in terms of form-as-process. But, given the as yet unbridged expressive gulf between the movement's sublime and pathetic music, too much remains to be done. The move-ment's expressive contrasts and formal ambiguities and tensions remain largely unresolved at the end. As Kramer argues, 'the presence of the problem does not necessarily mandate a solution'.[9] What roles, then, do the sonata's last two movements fulfil in response to this unfinished business?

Adagio

In contrast with the first movement, the Adagio fits very comfortably into a conformational model, namely 'slow-movement form', a sonata form in which the development section is replaced by a short retransi-tion passage back to the tonic.

Exposition	Theme 1	bars 1–17[1]
	Transition	17–30
	Theme 2	31–8[1]
	Retransition	38–42
Recapitulation	Theme 1	43–59[1]
	Transition	59–72
	Theme 2	73–80[1]
	Retransition	80–8
Coda	Theme 1, second period	89–98[1]
	Appendix	98–103

Figure 6.5 formal outline of Op. 31/2 Adagio

Nevertheless, in common with the first movement, several aspects of the music invite the perception of form as an unfolding process. For example, the opening thematic statement is richer in what it implies, rather than in what it actually contains. The first five bars are strikingly empty, and – given the large registral gaps between the bass chords and the unaccompanied treble responses – disjointed. Indeed the opening seems more like the skeleton of an idea than a fully elaborated presentation. And as the movement progresses, these implications are more fully realised with each reprise of the theme. At the opening of the movement, a sustained melodic line is achieved only at bar 6, leading to a half close at bar 8. The second period (bars 9–17) is more elaborate than the first, incorporating imitation of the ascending three-note figure, and rising to a peak of dissonance at bar 12. Within this period, the concept of a melodic process becomes ever more apparent, as when Beethoven plays a subtle game with the dissonant pitches in the last four bars of the theme. Bar 12 consists of two dissonant chords: a minor ninth (beat 1) and a seventh supporting $g\flat^1$ (beat 3). In the following bars both chords are resolved. The minor ninth loses its root to become a diminished seventh at bar 14^3, setting up a sequential chain of dissonances and resolutions that leads to B♭ in bar 16. Meanwhile the motive $g\flat^1$–f^1 at bars 12^3–13^1 is 'corrected' to $g\natural^2$–f^2 at bars 15–16.

The transition section begins over a B♭ pedal, the drum-like bass contrasting with the *legato* of the upper voices. In bars 18–19 Beethoven incorporates the chromatic turning figure ($e\flat^1$–d^1–$c\sharp^1$–d^1) that was subjected to so much violence in the first movement. A sudden move to a C major chord in bars 22–3 initiates a V/V pedal and, in the treble, the slow unfolding of a sixth ($e\natural^1$ to c^2, bars 23–7) in preparation for theme 2.

In contrast to the opening of the movement, theme 2 epitomises a more conventionally classical lyricism. Its melodic line is more fluent, almost completely diatonic, and its periodic structure consists of two complementary four-bar phrases. At the same time, it has strong motivic connections the first movement's recitative passages: its c^2–d^2–c^2 head-motive recalls the $\hat{5}$–$\hat{6}$–$\hat{5}$ patterns of bars 144–5 and 154–6, and its characteristic rhythm compresses bar 145. Unlike theme 1, theme 2 does not close strongly. Instead, the treble descends through an F chord to a ($\hat{3}$) in bars 37–8, leading to the more bitter dissonances of the retransition. In bar 38 the drum-like bass returns as an F pedal, while the treble slowly unfolds through a minor ninth chord (the most dissonant element in theme 1), reaching its apex at $e\flat^2$ in bar 42, then resolving to B♭ at the start of the reprise in bar 43.

In the recapitulation theme 1 is subjected to a series of fantasy-like variation processes. The first period (bars 43–50) is intensified by the incorporation of imitation and minor ninths (derived from bars 9–14), and the second period (bars 51–9) is veiled in more luxuriant figuration. While the demisemiquavers may have the primary functions of creating a wash of sound and of bridging the theme's registral gaps, they may also be heard as a transformation of elements from the first movement: the Largo's spread chords, and the Allegro's broken-chord diminished sevenths (in bars 52–4 and 182–4).

The transition section is altered to accommodate the new tonal structure. Its chromatic turning figure (bar 60 onwards) now begins on a♭, leading to the subdominant in bar 63, and thence to an F pedal at bar 65. Similarly, the retransition at the end of the reprise veers towards the subdominant (bars 81–5), before cadencing in B♭ at bar 89. Though the coda resolves the retransition's dissonances, it behaves more like a peroration than a climactic goal. It begins with yet another variation of the second period from theme 1. If, at the start of the reprise in bar 43, the first period was varied in the more elaborate manner of the second, now the second period reappears in the simplified manner of the first. Its registral gaps are widened, as in the juxtaposition of A^1 and c^3 in bars 92–3, and the more elaborate decorative figures are pared away. The six-bar appendix (bars 98–103) turns to a more conventional lyricism, though the movement's characteristic minor ninths are echoed by the C♭ passing notes in bars 98 and 100. In the remarkable closing bar, the registral gap between the treble and bass is again opened up, and the final treble gesture ($\hat{3}$–$\hat{2}$–$\hat{1}$) anticipates the opening of the finale.

As Kramer remarks, the most obvious point of contact between the first and second movements is the former's recitative passages. The Adagio develops their pathetic sensibility, and derives much of its materials from their constituent motives. Yet, as this account has attempted to show, the slow movement also appropriates motives from the Allegro's *Sturm und Drang* sections, especially in the many transition passages. Rather than attempting a synthesis of the first movement's expressive contrasts, the Adagio inverts the Allegro's expressive contrasts: the sublime becomes subsidiary to sentimentality.

Allegretto

While the finale engages primarily with the first movement's *Sturm und Drang* and motoric characteristics, it presents a more thorough synthesis of sentiment and the sublime than the Adagio. Likewise, the tensions between the conformational and generative aspects of form are more evenly balanced. Despite its moderate tempo marking, the finale's phrase structure is based on groups of hypermeasures rather than of individual bars. The basic unit of organisation is the four-bar hypermeasure, but Beethoven characteristically treats this with flexibility. For instance, the first theme ends with a two-bar group (bars 29–30), and the exposition's closing theme involves metrical expansion and contraction (six-bar units in bars 67–78, then four-bar units from bar 79 onwards). There is a plastic, dynamic relationship between foreground details and the larger patterns that underpin them. Sometimes Beethoven stresses the underlying processes, at other times expressive detail appears paramount, and – of course – subtle connections between the two layers abound. In the first theme, for example, bars 0–8 outline a leisurely treble ascent from d^2 to f^2 (thereby reversing the pattern of the first four semiquavers). Next the treble seems repeatedly to strive for some unattainably high goal, before sinking back each time to its original level. In bar 8 it grasps at d^3, but in the following three bars it falls back through a series of thirds (with a Neapolitan bass inflection in bar 10), before cadencing on d^2 at bar 15. Again in bar 16 it grasps (now more urgently) at d^3, again it sinks in the subsequent bars. So far the larger picture has been more significant than the affective foreground detail, despite the expressive intensity of details like the juxtaposed E♭ and A chords in bars 10–11. However, in the theme's closing period the details claim far more attention: the semiquaver *perpetuum mobile* is disrupted by two octave leaps in the treble, the first from a^1 to a^2 (bar 23) and the second from d^2 to d^3 (bar 27). And both these upward 'striving' gestures are answered by chromatic melodic descents in bars 24 and 28. Thus the foreground details can be perceived here as a reflection of the theme's underlying patterns. Finally, Beethoven's treatment of the highest treble note, d^3, illustrates a more complex interaction of musical detail and underlying form. In each successive striving gesture, d^3 shifts forward towards a metrically stronger part of the bar: from the last semiquaver (bar 8), to the last quaver (bar 16), the second quaver (bar 27), and eventually – at the very end of theme in bar 31 – to the beginning of the bar.

At the theme's final cadence, the treble's melodic close on d^3 is elided with the start of the transition passage. While Beethoven has hitherto checked the theme's tendency to become angry, the full rage of the *Sturm und Drang* style is unleashed here. The head-motive is taken into the lowest possible bass register at bar 30, leading to a d–G^7–C progression over the next eight bars. This pattern begins to repeat a tone lower from bar 38, but in bar 42 the seventh chord on F is replaced by its enharmonic equivalent, an augmented sixth, which resolves to E (V/V) in the next bar.

The wrench to V/a breaks the established thematic pattern, and the next twenty-five bars seem to return to the processual style of the first movement. Beginning on an unstable first-inversion dominant in bar 43, the music makes repeated attempts to close, but closure is compromised by elision (bar 51), and thwarted by interruption (bars 59 and 63). Although the period concludes with a perfect cadence at bar 67, even this is undermined by the sudden drop from *forte* to *piano*. Motivically, too, this section looks back to the first movement, with its melodic emphasis on $\hat{6}$–$\hat{5}$ patterns (f^2–e^2 in bars 43–8, etc.). There is, however, a stronger relationship between bars 43–51 and the Allegretto's head-motive: the repeated f^2–e^2 motive makes an obvious reference to the anacrusis in bar 0; more subtly, in bars 47–51 the treble fills in the leap from a^1 to f^2 which launched the movement. Closure having been achieved in bar 67, the rest of the exposition repeats A minor cadences and builds up to a ferocious *Sturm und Drang* climax at bar 87. A diminished seventh on C♯ swings the music back towards D minor at bar 91, and in the next four bars the treble climbs through the sixth a^1–f^2 to lead back to bar 1.

Beethoven's most striking compositional experiment in the development section is his unrelenting focus on a single rhythmic pattern. Variety stems from the larger patterns created by contrasts in texture, dynamics, pitch motives, and harmonic pacing. In broad terms the development may be interpreted as a slow neighbour-note progression (Example 6.6), moving from A at the end of the exposition to B♭ minor

Example 6.6 Op. 31/2/iii Harmonic outline of the development section

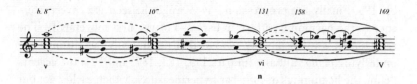

(bars 131–60) and back to A (=V/d) at bar 169. This plan is elaborated into four distinct sections.

(1) (bars 85–110) Four-bar hypermeasures of *piano* and *forte* alternate. Sequentially, diminished sevenths are created and resolved, supported by an ascending chromatic bass (f#–a) that takes the music through G minor to A minor.

(2) (bars 110–50) From bars 110–34 the texture changes every eight bars: first the bass leads (bars 110–18), next the treble (bars 118–26), and so on. As in section 1, diminished sevenths are created and resolved. Though the arpeggio figures give the bass a greater mobility here, they are underpinned by a slower bass descent in whole tones from g to d♭, passing through D minor and C minor to B♭ minor. In bars 134–50 B♭ minor is grounded as a local tonic as the bass rises from d♭ to b♭. From bar 143 the harmony changes every two bars, and there is a *crescendo* to *fortissimo*, driving the music towards its next goal, the start of the third section.

(3) (bars 150–73) With a sudden drop to *piano* the main theme is reprised in B♭ minor. But after eight bars the bass seems to get stuck on B♭, while the treble rises chromatically from f² to g#², producing an augmented sixth in bar 168. This resolves to A in the next bar, and is followed by a series of imperfect cadences, all marked with off-beat *sforzati*.

(4) (bars 173–214) The retransition – essentially a V upbeat to the recapitulation – is unusually long and harmonically rich. Both characteristics are in part prompted by the need to dissipate the extreme structural dissonance of the B♭ minor section. Beethoven's chief method of lowering harmonic tension is to include subdominant inflections in bars 181–8 and bars 191–2, though they also have the paradoxical effect of maintaining a certain restlessness on the surface of the music. (The nods towards G minor tie together various features of the development, reprising the f♯–g bass progression from bars 95–9, and keeping B♭ in play as a melodic pitch: a vital component in the lead up to the climax at bar 199. Finally, the progression i–iv–V might be seen as a covert reference to the harmonic pattern in bars 2–5 of the first movement.) The restlessness is intensified by *sforzati* that periodically cut through the underlying *piano*. Initially (in bars 179, 183, 187, and 191) the accents define the beginnings of four-bar hypermeasures, which earlier got out of synchronisation with harmonic goals in bars 167–9. But, in the course of the retransition, the accents acquire an extra expressive force, pushing the music towards its V^9 climax at bar 199. Finally, in bars 199–214 swirling hemiola figures outline a broad diminished seventh chord, threatening to lead to a *Sturm und Drang* apotheosis of the main theme. A sudden *piano* in bar 211 deflates those expectations, and the recapitulation starts not with a bang but a whimper.

The main theme proceeds as normal until bar 232 where, echoing the design of the development section, it gravitates towards B♭. Typically, the transition section (bar 242 onwards) embraces a wider tonal range than in the exposition. It begins with a shift to B♭ minor, proceeding through a rising circle of fifths (b♭–f–c–g) until, at bars 270–1, an augmented sixth on B♭ resolves to A (=V/i). The rest of the recapitulation mirrors the exposition. Similarly, the start of the coda parallels the start of the development, with a chromatic bass ascent from f♯ to a. But from bar 335 the bass is stabilised on the dominant, and supports free-floating chromatic decorations in the treble. While the pedal accumulates harmonic tension, the dynamics ebb and flow, falling to *pianissimo* at bar 349. An apotheosis of the main theme follows in bar 350: for eight bars it maintains an impassioned *fortissimo* with off-beat accents, before dropping back to *piano*. But Beethoven reserves a final outburst for the end: to the two closing octave leaps from a^2 and d^3 he adds a third, *fortissimo* from the top note of his piano (f^3) in bar 381. This is indeed a powerfully climactic gesture, though the finality of the subsequent cadence (bars 384–5) is undermined by its sudden *piano*. The last fifteen bars liquidate the movement's basic motive: perfect cadences (bars 385–93) give way to a tonic pedal, and in the last three bars the music fades away through an unaccompanied arpeggio falling to D.

In comparison with the rather superficial connections between the outer movements of the G major Sonata, the movements of this sonata are more profoundly integrated. Not only are there clear motivic links between all three movements, but they are related to one another by an overarching expressive process: the progression sublime-sentiment-synthesis. Additionally, the contrasts between generative and conformational forms in the first two movements give way to something approaching an equilibrium in the finale.

No. 3 in E♭

Allegro

The last sonata in Op. 31 synthesises the most engaging aspects from nos. 1 and 2. Its expressive domain harks back to the wit and brilliance of the G major Sonata, but these qualities have been deepened by Beethoven's experience of writing the 'Tempest'. Many of the D minor Sonata's radical technical experiments leave their mark here, though transformed with a comedic lightness of touch. And the main idea of the E♭ sonata appears to grow from and to complement a striking feature from the 'Tempest' sonata. In the D minor Sonata's first movement, the off-tonic opening initiated a structure in which closure was continually postponed. But in the E♭ Sonata Beethoven uses an off-tonic opening as the starting point for a sustained exploration of the stereotyped closing gestures found in late-eighteenth-century music.

Kofi Agawu, discussing the musical devices that signal the end of a section or movement in the classical style, has made a useful distinction between the syntactic and rhetorical aspects of closure.[10] In eighteenth-century music the syntax of closure is very simple: a perfect cadence, usually supporting a melodic descent from $\hat{2}$ to $\hat{1}$. But in the classical period, opening ideas also usually end with a perfect cadence. How, then, are endings to be distinguished from beginnings? Apart from the obvious temporal arrangement (beginnings begin, endings end), what makes endings distinctive is their rhetorical component: the presentational strategies – especially repeated phrases, motives, and cadences – that *emphasise* closure. Because the classical attitude towards closure was so stylised, composers could treat it as a topic for musical discourse, and even substitute beginnings for endings and *vice versa*. In Ratner's words, 'the very conventionality of a gesture allows it . . . to be put "out of countenance"'.[11] This is exactly what Beethoven does in Op. 31 no. 3. The *opening* theme has all the conventional signs of closure: it is a cadential progression; it contains motivic repetition from bar to bar, and the whole period is immediately given a varied repeat (bars 10–17); most importantly, it makes a point of its ending, since it derives its meaning from the search for closure in E♭.

Beyond the general rhetorical conventions, there were further 'vocabularies' of closure associated with specific genres. In this Allegro Beethoven particularly uses the brilliant style associated with closure in concertos and bravura arias. The solo sections in Mozart's piano concertos usually end climactically with brilliant figuration – semiquaver scales and broken chords to the top of the keyboard – and with the *sine qua non* of concerto closure, an extended cadential trill. Additionally, Mozart often approaches his final cadence with a slowly rising bass line supporting chromatic harmonies.[12] One of Beethoven's most original strokes here is the way he separates these syntactic and generic components: the movement opens in a lyrical minuet style, and the brilliant style is reserved for the later stages of the exposition.

Like the opening of the D minor Sonata, the Allegro's first sixteen bars embody the characteristics of statement (a double presentation of the main theme) and introduction (they form a tonal upbeat to the E♭ pedal in bar 17). A similar duality affects the following period (bars 17–25): with its *Trommelbaß* tonic pedal it sounds like a conventional opening idea, but it also acts as a transition, developing motives from bars 1 and 7–8. However, if this is music in the process of 'becoming', it lacks the D minor Sonata's intense harmonic dynamism. The first theme's cadential structure and the variation processes that govern bars 1–16 highlight parataxis (the element of segmentary repetition) rather than long-term symphonic energy (see Figure 6.6).

Period		Bars
1	Lyrical minuet IV^6_5–7^0–V^6_4–$^5_3$–I	1–9
2	Variation of Period 1	10–17
3	Extended IV–I cadences over I pedal	17–25
4	I–V, based on motive from bar 8	25–32
5	Pathetic, minor-mode development of Period 1 ($\rightarrow$ V/V)	33–45

Figure 6.6 Op. 31 no. 3: periodic structure of the first group

Example 6.7 Op. 31/3/i First and second themes

The tonic's stranglehold is weakened by the broad imperfect cadence in period 4. But it takes the move to E♭ minor in bar 33 to inject the tonal dynamic with real momentum: the minor mode introduces a degree of instability which allows the subsequent modulation to B♭. A sequence of two-bar figures ascends from E♭ minor to F minor in bars 35–42, and the 7^0 in bar 42 resolves chromatically (via an augmented sixth) to F major (V/B♭) in bar 44. The lyrical-pathetic style of bars 33–43 is abruptly snapped by octave leaps covering the whole of the keyboard in bars 44–5, a gratuitously inflated gesture that introduces the sharper wit of the second group.

While the second subject's brilliant style contrasts with the first subject's lyricism, its materials are clearly derived from the opening eight bars (Example 6.7). It begins with a weakly articulated tonic (in first inversion) and progresses towards a perfect cadence. Its motives include the falling fifth from bar 1 and three-note chromatic ascents. The linking scale from bars 8–9 is also transformed into an absurdly long, circular linking passage in bars 53–6. Moreover, the second subject's variation form (bars 46–53 varied in bars 57–64) echoes the repetitive aspects of the first group. Beethoven further explores brilliant-style closure in the continuation of the second subject (bars 64ff.): in bars 67–71 trills decorate cadences on different degrees of the scale, and from bar 72 the rate of harmonic change slows considerably, while broken chords and a long terminal trill dominate the figuration. Following the main perfect cadence at bar 82, the music returns to the lyrical minuet style of the start. An emphasis on the local subdominant (E♭) in bars 83–4 is used to prepare the exposition repeat, so that bars 87–91 outline a I–IV$^6_5$ progression in E♭.

The movement's off-tonic opening fundamentally affects the shape of the development section in at least three ways. First, in common with the first-movement developments in the other Op. 31 sonatas, this section takes its starting point from the opening of the exposition. But, since the sonata began with a dissonant chord (IV$^6_5$), its return in bar 89 cannot be considered as a lowering of harmonic tension. Rather, it is a matter of the music retracing its steps to obtain a better launch-pad for the subsequent modulation to C major (bar 100). Second, the off-tonic opening affects the development's ultimate harmonic goal. In the classical era the 'normal' goal of a sonata-form development is the V–I cadence at the start of the recapitulation. But here the goal is the dissonant chord with which the movement began. Third, two tonal regions are stressed by Beethoven's design: C major forms a stable subsidiary tonic in bars 100–14, and F minor is highlighted (bars 130–5) in preparation for the recapitulation. Thus the two dissonant melodic pitches from bar 1 are transformed into significant harmonic areas in the development.

In contrast to its unusual tonal design, the development's motivic processes pursue classical patterns of fragmentation and liquidation with exemplary clarity. Bars 89–99, returning to the movement's opening ideas, behave like a modulating transition to the C major theme at bar 100. From bar 109 the theme's components are broken down and interspersed with brilliant outbursts derived from bars 64–5 and bar 72 onwards. Finally, even this exchange of ideas is liquidated as the harmony gravitates towards F minor in bars 128–30, leaving only an arpeggio derived from the bass pattern of the previous bars.

At the start of the recapitulation the opening theme's new context obviously invests it with new meanings. If the off-tonic opening was bizarre at the start of the movement, it is now harmonically necessary for the return to E♭. Although the thematic reprise begins at bar 137, the strongest point of tonal resolution into the tonic arrives at bar 153 with the launch of the *Trommelbaß* period. In the recapitulation, Beethoven alters the first group to accommodate the new tonal pattern: he cuts the modulating minor-mode period, and the fourth period's imperfect cadence provides sufficient preparation for the second group. The second group, now in E♭, closely follows the pattern of the exposition, though Beethoven plays with registral levels in the treble, caps the absurdity of the brilliant linking passage (bar 53 onwards) by extending it from four to six bars (bar 177 onwards), and becomes even more obsessive with cadential trills (bars 67–71).

The coda raises a fundamental compositional problem that arises directly from Beethoven's materials. Since the whole movement has been 'about' closure, how is the composer to achieve a sense of an ending here? Joseph Kerman has suggested that around 1800 a general principle informs Beethoven's sonata-form codas: an 'aberration' in the first theme is removed in the coda with 'a thematic function that can be described . . . as "normalisation", "resolution", "expansion", "release", "completion", and "fulfilment"'.[13] In this Allegro the first theme has two 'aberrations': it lacks a harmonically stable opening, and it closes too emphatically. Yet none of Kerman's terms realistically apply to the composer's treatment of the theme at the end of the movement. Typically, Beethoven approaches the coda with a gesture that parallels the transition from the exposition to development: a move to the local subdominant, A♭, in bar 218. The first theme's chromatic ascent, beginning from the 'wrong' place in bar 222, simply continues rising until it reaches the 'correct' goal (I^6_4) at bar 233. As at the start of the recapitulation, the first theme here acquires a new meaning, since it is now has the function of recapturing E♭ major. But the aberration of the off-tonic opening is hardly removed: if anything, it is intensified. Nor is the rhetoric of closure made appreciably more forceful in the following bars. The closing eight-bar period, based on a subsidiary idea from bar 8, seems to shrug off the problem of false endings versus the true end, rather than addressing it squarely. This coda, for all its wit, is provisional. Beethoven reserves his forceful solution for the finale.

Scherzo: Allegretto vivace

There is a remarkable consistency of tone in this sonata. Instead of placing a slow movement here he follows the wit of the Allegro with a sonata-form scherzo of high originality: a march which is by turns jaunty, sly, and raucous, and which achieves in places a Mendelssohnian gossamer lightness.

As in the opening theme of the first movement, the Scherzo's main theme immediately emphasises C and F in bars 1–2. And, as in the first movement, these two pitches later come to assume a fundamental structural importance. The potential for the music to move towards F is raised as early as bar 10, where *pianissimo* octaves begin to outline a C^7 chord, inviting a resolution to F. A teasing *ritardando* in bars 13–15 stretches such expectations. But the subsequent resolution avoids F, moving instead to a V^7 chord on E♭ (bars 18–19) and then to a reprise of the main theme in A♭ (bar 20). Thus the whole process begins again, and the second time around Beethoven allows the music to fulfil its potential, cadencing into F major at bar 35. The following sixteen bars outline a broad circle of fifths, moving from F to B♭ (bar 39) and eventually cadencing in E♭ at bar 50. The remaining twelve bars of the exposition ground this key with a series of perfect cadences. On the surface of the music this tonal drama is articulated by a series of four themes that are differentiated as much by rhythmic patterns as by contrasting pitch shapes. For example, theme 1 (bars 1–9) and theme 3 (bar 35 onwards) are characterised by fluent semiquaver motion, while theme 2 (bars 10–19) has more disjointed patterns. The dotted rhythms of the repeated-note figures in bars 13–17 return in the bass at bar 43 and in the treble at theme 4 (bar 50), dominating the later stages of the exposition.

At the end of the exposition (bars 59–62) the top voice rises in semitones to return to the opening, but when the exposition is repeated this is imitated in bars 61–4 by a chromatically ascending bass which takes the music from E♭ to F major. While F formed a passing chord during the modulation to E♭ in the exposition, at the start of the development it momentarily becomes a stable tonic for a reprise of the main theme (bars 64–9). Significantly the theme's *sforzati*, which emphasised f^1 in bar 2, are missing now that F has been transformed from a melodic detail to a temporary tonic. But Beethoven side-steps an emphatic closure in F: the theme is open ended, and dissolves into theme 3 at bar 70. Cadences in B♭ minor and C minor lead to a second reprise of the main theme, now in C major (bar 83). Once more strong closure is avoided. From bar 87 the treble ascends from e♮^{2} through a diminished seventh to d♭^{3} at bar 90. In the following bars the diminished seventh chord is transformed into a dominant seventh on E♭ by a chromatic shift (e♮–e♭), and the recapitulation is introduced by a comically drawn-out scale descending through four and a half octaves, from d♭^{3} to A♭^{1} in bars 100–6.

The recapitulation largely follows the plan of the exposition, though modifications in bars 138–48 bring about a close in the tonic and play off against expectations created earlier in the movement. Instead of the expected F major chord in bar 140, Beethoven substitutes octave D♭s, taking the music temporarily to G♭. This gesture is repeated a tone higher at bar 144, taking the music to A♭ and completing an ascending third C (bar 138)–D♭ (bar 140)–E♭ (bar 144), which expands the movement's head-motive. Themes 3 and 4 follow in A♭, and from bar 163 a brief coda – played entirely in octaves – gives a parting summary of the main theme, embedded in running semiquavers.

Menuetto: Moderato e grazioso

Although its style was becoming increasingly archaic Beethoven intermittently returned to the moderately paced minuet throughout his career, from the numerous examples in the 1790s through to the Eighth Symphony (1812) and the last of the 'Diabelli' Variations (1823). Why did this type of minuet hold its fascination for him? A comparison between this sonata and the Symphony suggests that formal considerations might have played a role: in both works a *scherzando* second movement is succeeded by a minuet, as though the slower third movement is made to compensate for the faster second. But the culminating variation of the 'Diabelli' set hints that the minuet had more profound generic attractions for Beethoven. It represents the ultimate transformation of the materials from Diabelli's waltz, the apotheosis of the musically commonplace in 'a kind of final spiritualized reminiscence'.[14] Yet, with its profusion of detailed figuration, its lyricism, and above all with its self absorption, this sounds quite unlike an authentic eighteenth-century minuet.

Similarly the style of this sonata's Menuetto is markedly at odds with the 'minuet style' of the first movement, indulging in an unbroken lyricism that is rare in classical minuets. Like its counterpart in the Eighth Symphony it projects long melodic lines that override harmonic articulation at the ends of phrases. It also modestly anticipates the transcendent qualities of the 'Diabelli' minuet with its lyrical contemplation of ideas that are treated dramatically elsewhere in the work: here the first two movements' preoccupation with the pitch c^2 and its chromatic variant $c\flat^2$. The first eight-bar section consists of a single melodic arch. It rises from the tonic to its apex at bars 5–6 – a figure oscillating between $b\flat^1$ and c^2 – before falling back to an imperfect cadence at bar 8. Bars 9–12 focus on the apex of the first phrase, but with a bittersweet substitution of $c\flat^2$ for c^2. The treble rises into a higher octave at the end of bar 12. Despite their varied figuration the last four bars make a formal rhyme with bars 5–8: the B♭–C motive returns, and bar 8's imperfect cadence is resolved with a perfect cadence at bar 16.

The Trio continues to dwell on the Menuetto's ideas, but in a decidedly more laconic manner. Having taken the entire Menuetto to rise through an octave, the treble now exceeds the leap in a single crotchet (g^1 to $a\flat^2$ in bars 16–17). Yet the first four bars outline the same arch shape as the opening of the Menuetto, its apex (c^2) emphasised with a *sforzato*. Similarly the minor ninth chord that supported $c\flat^2$ in bar 9 becomes the sole chord of the Trio's central section (bars 25–30) before C♮ reasserts its predominance in bar 33. However, the conflict between C♮ and C♭ has yet to be worked through. Following a reprise of the Menuetto an eight-bar Coda returns the treble to its low starting point and liquidates the movement's opening rhythm. And in a sinister move that recalls bar 33 in the first movement, F♭ and C♭ replace their major-mode counterparts until they too are liquidated, leaving just the tonic, *pianissimo*.

Presto con fuoco

After the courtly finesse of the Menuetto has faded away, the sonata concludes with a furious virtuoso tarantella in sonata form. This finale has a symphonic momentum which is every bit as powerful as the first movement of the D minor Sonata. And, like the opening movement of the 'Tempest', some of its themes appear to be the products of underlying musical processes, rather than 'finished' musical objects in their own right.

The Presto con fuoco returns to the first movement's preoccupation with the rhetoric of closure, but problematises the issues more acutely.

While the opening theme of the first movement outlined a process of tonal closure by starting away from the tonic, the finale's first theme is more brutally obsessed with cadences. This theme is all 'end', and has gaping holes where there should be a beginning and middle. Its beginning consists only of the accompaniment, a bizarre type of Alberti bass that incorporates accented dissonant neighbour notes and is comically out of synchronisation with the bar line. As a result B♭ is accented and the tonic chord appears in its weakest position. The 'middle' consists of an isolated closing shape (cadencing onto Î) in the treble, but the cadence is unco-ordinated with the bass, so that its closure is cancelled out by its supporting B♭ (bar 4). Finally in bars 5–6 the treble and bass are co-ordinated at a perfect cadence. Beethoven repeats this baffling process in its entirety before the movement's main harmonic business begins at bar 13.

Theme 2 (bars 13–28) is a variation of the Menuetto's first eight bars: an arch shape ascending from e♭¹ to an apex on c²–b♭¹ (bars 21–2) before falling back to e♭¹ at bar 28. At bar 29 C♭ substitutes for C♮ (from bar 21), and in bar 33 a further chromatic variant – introducing A♮ and C♮ – takes the music to V/V. Having made the crucial move to establish B♭ as a subsidiary tonic, Beethoven now takes time to cadence strongly into the key, drawing out the process until bar 64. Indeed the rest of the exposition is solely concerned with the process of closing in B♭. Theme 4 – built from neutral arpeggio figures – merely grounds the new tonic until bar 76, where an ascending third in the treble reintroduces a♭, creating a dominant seventh for the exposition repeat.

If the exposition had a fairly circumscribed harmonic range, Beethoven blows it wide open in the development section. At the second-time bar the sudden reappearance of A♭ seems to spark off associations with C♭ from bar 29, and the treble rises through another third, arriving on a D♭⁷ chord at bar 82. A perfect cadence at bar 84 ushers in theme 2 in the remote key of G♭ major. But before this has a chance to settle it is enharmonically transformed into F♯ and initiates a series of perfect cadences: first in B minor (bars 91–8), second in C minor (bars 100–4). Now, for the third time in this sonata, C functions as a significant tonal area in a development section. A i–VI–♭II⁶–V⁷ progression in c is outlined in bars 104–20, followed by a reprise of theme 2 in C major (bars 120–7). This gives way to a stretch of two-part invertible counterpoint, spinning through a series of diminished sevenths and minor ninths to outline a flatward circle of fifths (bars 127–43). The strong momentum of this passage leads to a momentous climax on A♭ at bar 148 (theme 5). Finally the bass descends in thirds, from A♭ to F (bars 152–9), D (bars 160–3), and B♭ (bar 164), covering a V⁷/E♭ in preparation for the recapitulation.

Classical sonata-form recapitulations accomplish tonal resolution most obviously by reprising in the tonic material which earlier appeared in other keys. But it has long been recognised that mere emphasis on the tonic is insufficient to counterbalance the tonal tensions of the exposition and development. And as the dimensions of movements increase, so does the danger of long sections in the tonic becoming monotonous. In the late eighteenth century composers sought to overcome these problems by expanding the harmonic range of the first group of themes or the transition section and introducing new areas of tonal instability. Charles Rosen has termed these 'secondary developments' which introduce 'allusions to the subdominant or to related "flat" keys'. Although they may be disruptive in the short term, they ultimately serve 'to make the return to the tonic more decisive' at the start of the second subject.[15] Beethoven takes the strategy much further in this sonata. Instead of recapitulating the second subject in the tonic, he takes the end of theme 2 towards the flat side of E♭ and themes 3 and 4 are reprised in G♭ major (♭III). Roger Kamien has suggested that the prolongation of G♭ 'is doubtless motivated by the striking cadence to G♭ major at the beginning of the development section'.[16] But the harmonic function of the chord is different in each case, and other possible motivations suggest themselves (Example 6.8). In the development G♭ is part of a chromatic progression leading from B♭ (bar 76) to C (bars 104–27): at bar 92 G♭ is notated enharmonically as F♯ and functions as V/b (bar 96). In the recapitulation, however, G♭ arises from a move to E♭ minor in bar 200 (reprising bars 29ff.). E♭ minor acts as a stepping stone from its *tonic* major (E♭) to its *relative* major (G♭). From bar 209 the recapitulation parallels the exposition, transposing it down a minor third, until at bar 250 theme 4 modulates back to E♭ minor. So, although G♭ is the local tonic for much of the recapitulation, at a deeper level it is 'nested' inside the global tonic minor. Its appearance could thus be seen as the massive expansion of a seemingly insignificant minor-mode inflection from bars 29–32. To these retrospective reasons for the tonicisation of G♭ may be added

Example 6.8 Op. 31/3/iv Tonicisation of G flat in the development and
recapitulation

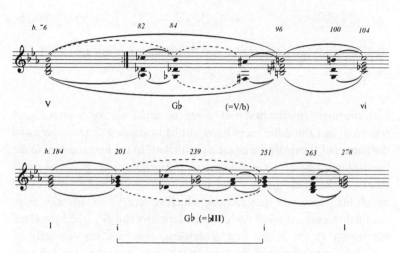

prospective motives, since Beethoven's strategy has a profound effect on the end of the sonata. Most obviously, strong tonal resolution is postponed to the end of the movement: a stylistic preoccupation of the Op. 31 set as a whole. There are also more subtle connections between the development, recapitulation and coda, connections which complement earlier aspects of the finale, and which ultimately bring the entire sonata full circle.

Like the development section, the recapitulation ends with a quiet dominant pedal (bars 263–78) which resolves to a weakly articulated tonic in bar 278 at the start of the coda. In the following bars theme 1's melodic fragments become the subject of a dialogue between the treble and bass, and the harmony moves from E♭ via F minor to A♭. This process reaches its climax with an allusion to theme 5 (from the development) in bar 303 onwards. After a diminished seventh chord in bars 307–8, the music cadences into E♭ with theme 1. On the surface of the music theme 1 has finally acquired the beginning and middle that it previously lacked. Underpinning the climax is a progression which reprises the very opening of the sonata (Example 6.9), the cadential pattern IV–7⁰–V–I. It also follows a similar dynamic pattern: motion towards a loud chord (held with a *fermata*) followed by a quiet resolution; and in

Example 6.9 Op. 31/3/iv Climax

both the finale and the first movement the entire phrase is immediately repeated. But the differences between the beginning of the sonata and the climax of the finale are equally significant. In the first movement the fermata emphasised a second-inversion E♭ chord with g¹ in the treble (bar 6); in the finale the fermata emphasises a diminished seventh chord which includes g♭¹, a modification which is hardly coincidental, given the finale's unusual tonal design. Furthermore, the g♭¹, which resolved incorrectly to g♮¹ in the first movement, now resolves correctly by descending to F (bar 309). Thus in these various ways the coda's climactic phrase becomes the *telos* of the entire sonata, not just its finale.

For the only time in Op. 31, cyclical connections between the outer movements are underlined with an affirmative, *fortissimo* ending. This brilliant, forceful, virtuosic reply to the earlier problem of closure appears truly heroic, all the more so in such a subversive, raucous context. Indeed, Op. 31 no. 3 was Beethoven's clearest formulation yet of the heroic paradigm that was to dominate his thinking for the next decade.

Notes

1 Keyboard culture

1 Mozart, Steibelt and Dussek did hold court appointments at various times in their careers, but only Steibelt's post at the Imperial Court in St Petersburg (from 1810) was long-term. None had the type of settled employment that Haydn enjoyed with the Ezsterházy family.

2 W. S. Newman, *The Sonata in the Classic Era* (Chapel Hill, 1963), pp. 48ff.

3 Beethoven's large concerts in the Vienna Burgtheater on 2 April 1800 and 5 April 1803 were exceptional in this respect.

4 For a sociological perspective on Beethoven's first decade in Vienna, see T. DeNora, *Beethoven and the Construction of Musical Genius: Musical Politics in Vienna, 1792–1803* (Berkeley, 1995), on whose arguments much of the following section rests.

5 On Beethoven's performing style, see G. Barth, *The Pianist as Orator: Beethoven and the Transformation of Keyboard Style* (Ithaca, 1992); and K. Komlós, *Fortepianos and their Music: Germany, Austria, and England 1760–1800* (Oxford, 1995).

6 DeNora, *Beethoven*, pp. 138ff.

7 Komlos, *Fortepianos*, pp. 143–4; DeNora, *Beethoven*, p. 129; and W. S. Newman, 'Beethoven's Pianos versus his Piano Ideals', *JAMS*, 23 (1970), p. 499.

8 DeNora, *Beethoven*, p. 159.

9 A. Stricher, *Kurze Bemerkungen über das Spielen, Stimmen und Erhalten der Fortepiano* (Vienna, 1801); see R. A. Fuller, 'Andreas Steicher's Notes on the Fortepiano – Chapter 2: "On Tone"', *Early Music*, 12 (1984), pp. 461–70 (with an English translation of the original German by P. de Silva).

10 Fuller, 'Andreas Streicher', pp. 464, 467.

11 Translation based on de Silva in Fuller, 'Andreas Streicher', pp. 467–8.

12 See Komlós, *Fortepianos*, pp. 24–30; Newman, 'Ideals'; and DeNora, *Beethoven*, pp. 174ff.

13 For more information on the construction of late-eighteenth-century

keyboard instruments, see Komlós *Fortepianos*, chapters 1 and 2; S. Rosenblum, *Performance Practices in Classical Piano Music: their Principles and Applications* (Bloomington, 1988), pp. 31ff; and M. N. Clinkscale, *Makers of the Piano 1700–1820* (Oxford, 1993).

14 Newman, 'Ideals', pp. 486, 487–8.

15 Newman, *ibid.*, pp. 491–8; Rosenblum, *Performance Practices*, pp. 121ff.

16 Letter of 19 November 1796; see E. Anderson (ed. and trans.), *The Letters of Beethoven* (London, 1961), I, p. 24.

17 Letter of 1796; Anderson, *Letters*, I, p. 25.

18 DeNora, *Beethoven*, pp. 177–8, 179.

19 For a detailed discussion of the generic, stylistic and sociological background to the genre, see Newman, *Sonata*.

20 See A. Ringer, 'Beethoven and the London Pianoforte School', *MQ*, 56 (1970), pp. 742–59; L. Plantinga, *Clementi: His Life and Music* (Oxford, 1977); O. L. Grossman, 'The Solo Piano Sonatas of Jan Ladislav Dussek', unpublished Ph.D. dissertation (Yale University, 1975).

21 DeNora, *Beethoven*, p. 179.

22 On the formation of a musical canon at the end of the eighteenth and beginning of the nineteenth centuries, see W. Weber, *The Rise of the Musical Classics in Eighteenth-Century England: A Study in Canon, Ritual and Ideology* (Oxford, 1992); and DeNora, *Beethoven*.

23 DeNora, *Beethoven*, pp. 11–36, deals with the influence of Baron van Swieten and Prince Lichnowsky in the creation of a receptive environment for 'serious' music.

24 For Nägeli's musical activities in general, see R. Hunziker, *H. G. Nägeli* (Zurich, 1938); for his connections with Beethoven, see M. Staehelin, *Hans Georg Nägeli and Ludwig van Beethoven: Der Züricher Musiker, Musikverleger und Musikschriftsteller in seiner Beziehungen zu dem grossen Komponisten* (Zurich, 1982).

25 *Allgemeine musikalische Zeitung*, 5/35 (25 May 1803).

26 *Ibid.*

2 Beethoven in 1800–1802

1 Anderson, *Letters*, I, p. 60.

2 *Ibid.*, pp. 64–5.

3 *Ibid.*, p. 67.

4 For a discussion of Beethoven's relationship with Countess Guicciardi, see Forbes, ed. and rev., *Thayer's Life of Beethoven* (hereafter, Thayer-Forbes), I, pp. 288–92.

5 F. Wegeler and F. Ries, *Biographisches Notizen über Ludwig van Beethoven* (1838), translated F. Noonan, as *Remembering Beethoven* (London, 1988), pp. 86–7.

6 For the complete text of the Heiligenstadt Testament in English translations, see M. Solomon, *Beethoven* (New York, 1977), pp. 116–18; and B. Cooper (ed.) *The Beethoven Compendium* (London, 1992), pp. 170–1.

7 R. Rolland, trans. E. Newman, *Beethoven the Creator: The Great Creative Epochs*, I, 'From the Eroica to the Appassionata' (London, 1929), p. 272.

8 *Ibid.*, p. 282.

9 Solomon, *Beethoven*, pp. 121, 124.

10 C. Wintle, 'Kontra-Schenker: Largo e Mesto from Beethoven's Op. 10 No. 3', *Music Analysis*, 4 (1985), pp. 148–9.

11 Beethoven, *Heiligenstadt Testament*, in Solomon, *Beethoven*, p. 118.

12 C. Czerny, *Errinerungen aus meinem Leben* (Strasbourg, 1968), p. 43.

13 Anderson, *Letters*, I, p. 76.

14 D. Johnson, '1794–1795: Decisive Years in Beethoven's Early Development', in A. Tyson (ed.), *Beethoven Studies III* (Cambridge, 1982), pp. 1-28: 27.

15 For discussions of tonally ambivalent openings in C. P. E. Bach and Haydn see S. L. F. Wollenberg 'A New Look at C. P. E. Bach's Musical Jokes', in S. L. Clark (ed.) *C. P. E. Bach Studies* (Oxford, 1988), pp. 295–314 (Keyboard Sonatas in F H.243, and B minor H.245); and G. A. Wheelock, *Haydn's Ingenious Jesting with Art: Contexts of Musical Wit and Humor* (New York, 1992), pp. 103–6 (String Quartet Op. 33 no. 1).

16 N. Marston, 'Stylistic Advance, Strategic Retreat: Beethoven's Sketches for the Finale of the Second Symphony', *Beethoven Forum*, 3 (1994), p. 150.

3 Composition and reception

1 G. Kinsky and H. Halm, *Das Werk Beethovens: Thematisch-bibliographisches Verzeichnis seiner sämtlichen vollendeten Kompositionen* (Munich, 1955), p. 102.

2 D. Johnson, A. Tyson and R. Winter (hereafter JTW), *The Beethoven Sketchbooks* (Oxford, 1985), p. 103.

3 *Ibid.*, pp. 109–10.

4 *Ibid.*, p. 113.

5 *Ibid.*, pp. 120–3.

6 *Ibid.*, p. 116.

7 A notice advertising Cappi's edition appeared in the *Wiener Zeitung* on 3 March 1802: see Kinsky-Halm, *Werk*, pp. 67–8.

8 Thayer-Forbes, I, p. 291.

9 On the basis of the postage times between Vienna and Zurich, JTW calculate that Beethoven might have received Nägeli's request some time in May 1802; JTW, *Sketchbooks*, p. 126.

10 T. Albrecht, ed. and trans., *Letters to Beethoven and Other Correspondence*, I, 1772–1812 (London, 1996), p. 70.

11 Albrecht, *Letters*, pp. 72, 73–5.

12 *Ibid.*, p. 77.

13 Wegeler-Ries, *Biographisches Notizen*, p. 76.

14 JTW, *Sketchbooks*, pp. 128, 133.

15 T. Albrecht, 'The Fortnight Fallacy: A Revised Chronology for Beethoven's *Christ on the Mount of Olives*, Op. 85, and the Wielhorsky Sketchbook', *Journal of Musicological Research*, 11 (1991), pp. 277–9.

16 La Mara, *Beethoven und die Brunsviks* (Leipzig, 1920), quoted in Staehelin, *Nägeli*, p. 24.

17 Kinsky-Halm, *Werke*, p. 79.

18 Wegeler-Ries, *Biographische Notizen*, pp. 77–8.

19 Albrecht, *Letters*, p. 102.

20 *Ibid.*, p. 103.

21 *Ibid.*, pp. 104–5.

22 *Ibid.*, p. 108.

23 *Ibid.*, p. 110.

24 See Ries's letter to Simrock on 13 September 1803; Albrecht, *Letters*, p. 114.

25 *Ibid.*, pp. 125–6.

26 Kinsky-Halm, *Werke*, p. 79.

27 Kinsky and Halm give May/June as the date of the earliest editions of the E♭ Sonata (*Werke*, p. 79). But Brandenburg suggests that, though an advertisement for a number of volumes of the *Répertoire des Clavecinistes* appeared in May and June 1804, volume 11 (containing Op. 31 no. 3) did not appear until November of that year (Seighard Brandenburg (ed.), *Ludwig van Beethoven: Briefwechsel Gesamtansgabe* I (1783–1807), (Munich, 1996), p. 233).

28 B. Cooper, *Beethoven and the Creative Process* (Oxford, 1990) p. 104.

29 Peter Hauschild has claimed that a short sketch in B minor from the Kafka sketchbook (f. 139), dating from 1799 at the latest, is an early concept sketch for the first movement of the C♯ minor Sonata (P. Hauschild, editorial introduction to L. van Beethoven, *Klaviersonate Op. 27/2*, Vienna, 1994, p. 6). But the draft contains only a few bars of triplet arpeggios with no tempo marking or added melodic layer, and seems hardly more than an all-purpose accompanimental pattern. Its connection with the sonata is tenuous.

30 See Cooper, *Creative Process*, pp. 188–90, and 'The Origins of Beethoven's D minor Sonata Op. 31 no. 2', *Music and Letters*, 62 (1981), pp. 261–80.

31 The term is Joshua Rifkin's: see Cooper, *Creative Process*, p. 105.

32 Cooper, *Creative Process*, p. 106.

33 Wielhorsky sketchbook, pp. 5 and 6.

34 The numbering of surviving leaves from the Sauer sketchbook follows JTW, *Sketchbooks*, pp. 120–1. The sketches given in chapter 3 were transcribed from facsimiles in H. Schenker, *Musikalischen Seltenheiten* (Vienna, 1927).

35 The table only contains synopsis sketches for the D minor Sonata. Cooper lists a larger number of concept sketches that relate to it; see Cooper, 'Origins'; and *Creative Process*, pp. 177–96.

36 Cooper, *Creative Process*.

37 Both sketches are in E♭. The first (headed 'Sonata II' on f. 93r staves 6 and 7) is in $\frac{4}{4}$ and, like the opening of Op. 31 no. 3, contains a chromatic ascending bass. In contrast with the finished sonata, however, the sketch begins firmly on the tonic chord. The second sketch is in $\frac{3}{4}$ and includes melodic turns of phrase that clearly anticipate bars 25 and 57–60 in the first-movement exposition of the finished sonata.

38 Thayer-Forbes, *Life*, pp. 339, 499, 659, 692 and 763.

39 H. Schmidt, editorial introduction to *Beethoven Werke*, VII, 3, ii (Duisburg, 1976), p. viii.

40 A. Tyson, *The Authentic English Editions of Beethoven* (Oxford, 1963), p. 43.

41 Brandenburg, *Briefwechsel*, p. 233.

42 Schmidt, *Werke*, p. viii. The main questions are: (1) who provided the *Stichvorlage*? and (2) to what extent do the English edition's variants with contemporaneous continental editions spring from editorial decisions in London, or from differences in the underlying sources?

43 For a discussion of Czerny's tempo indications see Sandra P. Rosenblum, 'Two sets of unexplored metronome marks for Beethoven's piano sonatas', *Early Music*, 16 (1988), pp. 59–71.

44 A. Tyson, 'Moscheles and his "Complete Edition" of Beethoven', *Music Review*, 25 (1964), p. 138. Tyson points out that Moscheles did not consult primary sources, but used whatever editions most readily came to hand, notably Hasslinger's edition from the late 1820s.

45 Statistic derived from W. S. Newman, 'A chronological checklist of Collected Editions of Beethoven's Solo Piano Sonatas since his own day', *Notes*, 33 (1977), pp. 503–30.

46 A. Schnabel, editorial introduction to L. van Beethoven, *32 Sonate per pianoforte* (Milan, 1993).

47 W. S. Newman, 'Liszt's Interpreting of Beethoven's Piano Sonatas', *Musical Quarterly*, 58 (1972), p. 203.

48 Steingräber worked under the pseudonym Gustav Damm in this edition.

49 The edition was revised by Erwin Ratz in 1945, and reprinted by Dover, with an extensive historical introduction by Carl Schachter, in the 1970s.

50 Volume VII, 3, II, containing Op. 27 and Op. 31, appeared in 1976. In Henle's two-volume offprint of this edition, Op. 27 is in volume I and Op. 31 in volume II.

51 Czerny, 'Anekdoten und Notizen über Beethoven', in *Über den richtigen Vortrag der sämmtlichen Wrke für das Piano allein*, ed. P. Badura-Skoda (Vienna, 1970), p. 13.

52 *AMZ*, 4/40 (30 June 1802), columns 651–3.

53 *Zeitschrift für die elegante Welt*, 3 (1803), column 611.

54 *Zeitschrift für die elegante Welt*, 7 (1807), column 70.

55 R. Hatten, *Musical Meaning in Beethoven: Markedness, Correlation and Interpretation* (Bloomington, 1994), p. 36.

56 Czerny, *Über den richtigen Vortrag*, pp. 43, 47.

57 *Ibid.*, p. 44.

58 H. Berlioz, 'Concerts [sic.] de M. Liszt', in *Journal des Débats*, 25 April 1835, quoted in Prod'homme, *Les Sonates pour piano de Beethoven (1782–1823): histoire et critique* (Paris, 1937), pp. 125–6.

59 W. Lenz, *Beethoven et ses Trois Styles*, p. 225.

60 Rellstab knew Beethoven and he was a fellow member with Schubert of the Ludlums Höhle club in Vienna (E. N. McKay, *Franz Schubert* (Oxford, 1996), p. 253). The song's last quatrain, linking moonlight with death and mourning, exemplifies a common yoking of the concepts in the early nineteenth century: see, for instance, the responses of Berlioz and Czerny to the Adagio sostenuto. For a broader cultural view, see M. Guiomar, *Principes d'une Esthétique de la Mort* (Paris, 1967), pp. 135–6, and (on Op. 27 no. 2 in particular) p. 154.

61 A. Schindler, trans. D. W. McArdle, *Beethoven as I Knew Him* (New York, 1966), p. 406.

62 The point is underlined by the numerous arrangements and transcriptions that have decontextualised the Adagio sostenuto, ignoring the strong telos that binds all three movements of the sonata together.

63 See L. Kramer, 'The Strange Case of Beethoven's *Coriolan*: Romantic Aesthetics, Modern Subjectivity, and the Cult of Shakerspeare', *MQ*, 79 (1995), pp. 256–80.

64 Schumann famously remarked that 'the German forgets in his Beethoven that he has no school of painting, with Beethoven he imagines that he has

reversed the fortunes of the battles he lost to Napoleon; he even dares to place him on the same level as Shakespeare' (*On Music and Musicians*, ed. K. Wolff, trans P. Rosenfeld (New York, 1969), p. 61).

65 See S. Burnham, 'The Role of Sonata Form in A. B. Marx's Theory of Form', *Journal of Music Theory*, 23 (1989), pp. 247–71.

66 A. B. Marx, *Die Lehre von der musikalischen Komposition: Praktisch-theoretisch*, III (Leipzig, 1845). For an English translation of relevant passages on sonata form, see A. B. Marx, trans. and ed. S. Burnham, *Musical Form in the Age of Beethoven: Selected Writings on Theory and Method* (Cambridge, 1997).

67 H. Riemann, *Ludwig van Beethoven sämtliche Klaviersonaten* (Berlin, 1919). Schenker published no detailed analysis of any of the Op. 27 or Op. 31 sonatas, though he did use the 'Moonlight' to illustrate several theoretical points in *Der freie Satz*.

68 K. L. Mikulicz, *Ein Notierungsbuch von Beethoven aus dem Besitz der Preussischen Staatsbibliothek zu Berlin* (Leipzig, 1927) [Landsberg 7]; S. Brandenburg, *Beethoven: Kesslerisches Skizzenbuch* (Bonn, 1976); N. Fishman, *Kniga eskizov Beethoven za 1802–1803 gody* (Moscow, 1962) [Wielhorsky].

69 W. S. Newman, 'Ideals'; Komlós *Fortepianos*; Barth *Pianist as Orator*; Rosenblum, *Performance Practices*.

70 Wegeler-Ries, *Notizen*, pp. 81–2.

71 Moscheles cited Czerny as an expert on good tempi for Beethoven's music: see Tyson, 'Moscheles', pp. 140–1.

72 Czerny, *Über den richtigen Vortrag*, pp. 24–5.

73 Newman, 'Liszt', p. 192.

74 *Revue musicale*, 9/15 (12 April 1835), pp. 115–16.

75 *Ibid.*, p. 116.

76 H. Berlioz, 'Trios et sonates', *Journal des Débats*, 12 April 1837, reprinted in *A travers chants* (Paris, 1862), pp. 62–4.

77 See T. Frimmel, *Beethoven-Forschung*, II (Vienna, 1928), p. 78; and Newman, 'Liszt', p. 191.

78 C. Engel, *The Pianist's Hand-book: a Guide for the Right Interpretation and Performance of our Best Pianoforte Music* (London, 1853), p. 164.

79 Cited in H. C. Schonberg, *The Great Pianists* (London, 1964), p. 221.

80 *Ibid.*, p. 236.

81 The recordings sampled are, in chronological order:

Ignaz Friedman	1926	(Pearl)
Frederick Lamond	1926	(HMV)
Artur Schnabel	April 1934	(EMI)
Solomon	1940s?	(HMV)

Walter Gieseking	1956	
Wilhelm Backhaus	1958	(Decca)
Rudolph Serkin	1963	(CBS)
Alfred Brendel	early 1970s	(Philips)
Emil Gilels	early 1980s	(DG)
Jos van Immerseel	1983	(Accent)
Steven Lubin	1989	(L'oiseau-lyre)
Malcolm Bilson	1996	(Claves)

4 *Quasi una fantasia?*

1 R. Schumann, '[Review of Berlioz: *Fantastic Symphony*]', *Neue Zeitschrift für Musik*, 3/9 (31 July 1835), p. 33.

2 See H. Dubrow, *Genre* (London, 1982).

3 H. R. Jauss, *Towards an Aesthetic of Reception* (London, 1982), pp. 79–80.

4 See Dubrow, *Genre*, especially pp. 1–7.

5 This has been termed the 'rhetoric of genre': see J. Kallberg, 'The Rhetoric of Genre: Chopin's Nocturne in G Minor', *Nineteenth-Century Music* II (1988), pp. 238–61.

6 On the other hand, it has been argued that a title is particularly relevant to the meaning of a work when it actively promotes ambiguity (J. Samson, 'Chopin and Genre', *Music Analysis*, 8 (1989), p. 217). A work whose genre is clear does not require an appropriate title to verify its status, but generic 'dissonance' between a work and its title might be richly allusive. The issue of whether the Op. 27 sonatas really are – in structuralist terms – '*quasi una fantasia*' is significant here.

7 H. C. Koch, *Kurzgefaßtes Handwörterbuch der Musik* (Leipzig, 1807), p. 146. Koch's article here was based on earlier ones in his *Musikalisches Lexicon* (1802) and the last volume of *Versuch einer Anleitung zur Compositions* (1793).

8 C. P. E. Bach, *Versuch über die wahre Art das Clavier zu spielen . . .* (Leipzig, 1753); trans. W. J. Mitchell as *Essay on the True Art of Playing Keyboard Instruments* (New York, 1949). The fifty-year gap between the appearance of Bach's treatise and Beethoven's sonatas does not affect its relevance: Beethoven probably encountered the *Versuch* when he was a pupil of Neefe at Bonn, and he later used it as a teaching manual (see Thayer-Forbes, *Life*, pp. 35 and 226–8).

9 Bach, trans. Mitchell, *Essay*, p. 438.

10 For a discussion of the 'symphonic' and 'sonata' styles in early Beethoven, see M. Broyles, 'The Two Instrumental Styles of Classicisim', *JAMS*, 36 (1983), pp. 210–42.

11 H. C. Koch, *Kurzgefaßtes Handwörterbuch*, p. 146.

12 D. G. Türk, trans. B. Haggh, *Essay*, p. 388.

13 P. Schleuning, *Der freie Fantasie: Ein Beitrag zur Erforschung der klassischen Klaviermusik* (Göppingen, 1973), part III, 'Der Ende der freien Fantasie', pp. 350–68.

14 For example, the piano trios Hob. XV nos. 24, 29 and 30.

15 For instance, pianos trios Hob. XV nos. 25, 27, 29, and 30; string quartets Op. 74 no. 3, Op. 76 nos. 5 and 6, Op. 77 nos. 1 and 2, and Op. 103; symphonies nos. 99, 103 and 104.

16 The string quartets Op. 76 nos. 5 and 6 eschew an opening sonata allegro, beginning instead with moderately paced movements whose forms combine rondo and variations. Consequently each quartet's centre of gravity is thrown forward on to the following slow movement (entitled 'Fantasia' in Op. 76 no. 6) and sonata allegro form is withheld until the finale.

17 J. Webster, *Haydn's 'Farewell' Symphony and the Idea of the Classical Style* (Cambridge, 1991), pp. 288–94.

18 See L. Ratner, *Classic Music: Expression, Form and Style* (London, 1980), p. 314; and K. Agawu, *Playing with Signs: A Semiotic Interpretation of Classic Music* (Princeton, 1991), p. 47.

19 See Ratner, *Classic Music*, pp. 310–12; and G. Wheelock *Haydn's Ingenious Jesting with Art*, pp. 37–54.

20 Ratner, *Classic Music*, pp. 312–14.

21 R. A. Kramer, 'Cadenza contra Text: Mozart in Beethoven's Hands', *Nineteenth-Century Music*, 15 (1991), pp. 116–31.

22 P. Schleuning, *Freie Fantasie*, pp. 350–5.

23 Few of Beethoven's earlier sonatas were published with unqualified titles. Works published alone under a single opus number were entitled 'Sonata grande', perhaps signifying pieces that Beethoven had written for his own use in salons (see Newman, *Sonata in the Classical Era*, p. 78). The composer and his publishers might also have kept a careful eye on market considerations: purchasers needed to be reassured that they were not being short-changed with a single sonata. The more specific descriptive title of Op. 13 – '*Grande Sonate pathétique*' – played on the contemporary vogue for the pathetic style and, by offering a guide (sight unseen) to the work's rhetoric and tone, undoubtedly boosted its early popularity (see E. R. Sisman, 'Pathos and the *Pathétique*: Rhetorical Stance in Beethoven's C minor Sonata, Op. 13', *Beethoven Forum*, 3 (1994), p. 81).

24 On the rise of the salon fantasy see Schleuning, *Der Freie Fantasie*. Of course, the rider '*quasi una fantasia*' might have functioned as a *caveat emptor*.

25 See R. Wallace, *Beethoven's Critics: Aesthetic Dilemmas and Resolutions during the Composer's Lifetime* (Cambridge, 1986), pp. 5–44.

26 Thayer-Forbes, *Life*, pp. 206–7.

27 Susan Wollenberg (in a private communication) points out that there is a remarkably consistent rhetorical style of writing about musical improvisation in the late eighteenth and early nineteenth centuries.

28 Thayer-Forbes, *Life*, p. 185.

29 J. Todd, *Sensibility: an Introduction* (London, 1986), pp. 30–1.

30 Thayer-Forbes, *Life*, p. 466.

31 Cited in Mies, 'Quasi una Fantasia . . .', in S. Kross and H. Schmidt, eds., *Colloquium Amicorum: Joseph Schmidt-Görg zum 70. Geburtstag* (Bonn, 1967) p. 242.

32 W. H. Wackenroder, *Herzergiessungen eines kunstliebendes Klosterbruders*, (1797).

33 C. Dahlhaus, trans. J. B. Robinson, *Nineteenth-Century Music* (Berkeley, 1989), p. 34.

34 Thayer-Forbes, *Life*, p. 164.

5 The design of the Op. 27 sonatas

1 C. Czerny, trans. and ed. A. L. Mitchell, *A Systematic Introduction to Improvisation on the Pianoforte*, Op. 200 (London, 1983), p. 74.

2 See L. Ratner, *Classic Music*, p. 14; M. E. Little, 'Gavotte' in S. Sadie, ed., *The New Grove Dictionary of Music and Musicians* (London, 1980), 7, pp. 199–202; and W.J. Allanbrook, *Rhythmic Gesture in Mozart* (Chicago, 1983), pp. 49–52.

3 See L. Ratner, *Classic Music*, p. 12; and W. J. Allanbrook, *Rhythmic Gesture*, pp. 59–60: the lower-class associations of the German dance are apparent in the Act I finale of Mozart's *Don Giovanni* (1787), where it is danced by the peasants Zerlina and Masetto. For a counterexample of this style in Beethoven's keyboard music, see the first movement of the G major Sonata Op. 79.

4 L. Ratner, *Classic Music*, p. 365.

5 *Ibid.*, p. 373.

6 A telling comparison can be made with the opening of the Adagio from the *Pathétique* Sonata Op. 13.

7 The Presto's thirds have a clear cyclical function too, since they recall the predominant interval of the opening Andante.

8 Haydn forges a similar link between the Minuet and Finale in his Symphony no. 46 in B (1774). The finale is interrupted towards the end of the recapitulation by a partial reprise of the minuet, providing melodic closure. See J. Webster, *Farewell*, pp. 262–80.

9 Nevertheless, the rapid succession of contrasting tempi alludes to the

pattern of movements that typically ended Viennese comic opera finales in the late eighteenth century, as – for example – in Act II of *Figaro* and Act II of *Don Giovanni*: see J. Platoff, 'Musical and Dramatic Structure in the Opera Buffa Finale', *JMus*, 7 (1989), pp. 191–230.

10 Even the unusual key of C♯ minor carried concrete connotations for Beethoven's contemporaries. In *Ideen zu einer Ästhetik der Tonkunst* (*c.* 1784), C. F. D. Schubart described the key as appropriate for the portrayal of 'penitential lamentation, intimate conversation with God . . . signs of disappointed friendship and love lie in its radius'. For J. H. Knecht (*Gemeinnütziches Elementarwerk*, 1792) it signified 'despair'; and for J. A. Schrader (*Kleines Taschenwörterbuch der Musik*, 1827) 'a depraved, insane mind and despair are expressed by the sharp sounds of this key'. Many later nineteenth-century discussions of the characteristics of C♯ minor cite Op. 27 no. 2. See R. Steblin, *A History of Key Characteristics in the Eighteenth and Early Nineteenth Centuries* (Ann Arbor, 1983).

11 E. J. Dent, *Mozart's Operas* (London, 1913), p. 141.

12 I. Krohn, 'Die Form des ersten Satzes der Mondscheinsonate', *Beethoven-Zentenarfeier* (Leipzig 1927), p. 58.

13 P. Benary, '*Sonata quasi una fantasia*: zu Beethovens Op. 27', *Musiktheorie*, 2 (1987), pp. 129–36.

14 Attributed to Liszt: see A. Ubilischeff, *Beethoven, seiner Kritiker und seiner Ausleger* (Berlin, 1859), p. 137.

15 This sonata's minor–major–minor pattern contrasts with the minor–major progression that characterises Beethoven's late two-movement sonatas, Op. 90 and Op. 111: see L. Kramer, *Music as Cultural Practice: 1800–1900* (Berkeley, 1990), pp. 21–71.

16 D.F. Tovey, *A Companion to Beethoven's Pianoforte Sonatas* (London, 1948), p. 112.

17 This off-tonic opening reworks the compositional strategy from the opening of the Menuetto in the A♭ Sonata Op. 26: see p. 16.

18 P. Mies, 'Quasi una Fantasia . . .', pp. 239–49.

6 The design of the Op. 31 sonatas

1 H. Riemann, *Beethovens sämtliche Klaviersonaten* pp. 320–1.

2 S. Burnham, 'A. B. Marx and the gendering of sonata form' in I. Bent, ed., *Music Theory in the Nineteenth Century* (Cambridge, 1996), p. 175.

3 Tovey, *Companion*, p. 122.

4 Tovey, *Companion*, p. 124.

5 O. Jander, 'Genius in the Arena of Charlatanry: The First Movement of

Beethoven's "Tempest" Sonata in Cultural Context', in *Musica Franca: Essays in Honor of Frank D'Accone* (New York, 1996), pp. 585–630.

6 L. Kramer, 'Primitive Encounters: Beethoven's "Tempest" Sonata, Musical Meaning, and Enlightenment Anthropology', in *The Beethoven Forum*, 6 (1998), pp. 31–66.

7 C. Dahlhaus, trans. M. Whittall, *Beethoven: Approaches to His Music* (Oxford, 1989), pp. 115–16.

8 J. Schmalfeldt, 'Form as the Process of Becoming: The Beethoven-Hegelian Tradition and the "Tempest" Sonata', *The Beethoven Forum*, 4 (1995), pp. 37–72.

9 Kramer, 'Primitive Encounters', p. 37.

10 K. Agawu, *Playing with Signs*, pp. 67–72.

11 Cited in J. Levy, 'Gesture, Form and Syntax in Haydn's Music' in J.P. Larsen and J. Webster, eds., *Haydn Studies* (New York, 1980), p. 356.

12 In the first movement of his E♭ Concerto K. 449 (1784) bars 162–9, and the Finale of the E♭ Concerto K. 482 (1785) bars 164–74, the harmonic progressions are functionally identical to the opening bars of Op. 31 no. 3.

13 J. Kerman, 'Notes on Beethoven's Codas', in A. Tyson, ed., *Beethoven Studies* (London, 1982), p. 149.

14 W. Kinderman, *Beethoven's Diabelli Variations* (Oxford, 1987), p. 125.

15 C. Rosen, *Sonata Forms*, p. 276.

16 R. Kamien, 'Aspects of the Recapitulation in Beethoven Piano Sonatas', *The Music Forum*, 4 (1976), pp. 195–236.

Select bibliography

Agawu, V. Kofi. *Playing with Signs: A Semiotic Interpretation of Classic Music* (Princeton 1991)

Albericht, Theodore. 'Beethoven and Shakespeare's *Tempest*: New Light on an Old Allusion', *The Beethoven Forum*, 1 (1992), pp. 81–92

Anderson, Emily. Trans. and ed., *The Letters of Beethoven*, 3 vols. (London 1961)

Barth, George. *The Pianist as Orator: Beethoven and the Transformation of Keyboard Style* (Ithaca 1992)

Bauer, E. E. *Wie Beethoven auf den Sockel kam: Die Entstehung eines musikalischen Mythes* (Stuttgart 1992)

Benary, P. '*Sonata quasi una fantasia*: zu Beethovens Op. 27', *Musiktheorie*, 2 (1987), pp. 129–36

Brandenburg, Sieghard. Ed., *Ludwig van Beethoven: Kesslerisches Skizzenbuch*, 2 vols., facsimile and transcription (Bonn 1976–8)

Broyles, Michael. 'The Two Instrumental Styles of Classicism', *Journal of the American Musicological Society*, 36 (1983), pp. 210–42

   Beethoven: the Emergence and Evolution of Beethoven's Heroic Style (New York 1987)

Burnham, Scott. *Beethoven Hero* (Princeton 1995)

   'A. B. Marx and the Gendering of Sonata Form', in *Music Theory in the Nineteenth Century*, ed. Ian Bent (Cambridge 1996), pp. 164–86

Cooper, Barry. 'The Origins of Beethoven's D minor Sonata Op. 31 no. 2', *Music and Letters*, 62 (1981), pp. 261–80

   Beethoven and the Creative Process (Oxford 1990)

Czerny, Carl. Ed. P. Badura-Skoda, *On the Proper Performance of all Beethoven's Works for the Piano* (Vienna 1970)

Dahlhaus, Carl. Trans. Mary Whittall, *Ludwig van Beethoven: Approaches to his Music* (Oxford 1989)

DeNora, Tia. *Beethoven and the Construction of Musical Genius: Musical Politics in Vienna, 1792–1803* (Berkeley and Los Angeles 1995)

Dubrow, Heather. *Genre* [*The Critical Idiom*: 42] (London 1982)

Select bibliography

Finscher, Ludwig. 'Beethovens Klaviersonate Opus 31, 3. Versuch einer Interpretation', *Festschrift für Walter Wiora* (Kassel 1967), pp. 385–96

Fischer, Edwin. *Ludwig van Beethovens Klaviersonaten*, Wiesbaden, 1956; Eng. trans. by S. Goodman and P. Hamburger, *Beethoven's Pianoforte Sonatas* (London 1959)

Fishman, Nathan L. Ed., *Kniga eskizov Beethovena za 1802–1803 gody*, ('Beethoven's Sketchbook from 1802–1803' (the 'Wielhorsky' Sketchbook)), 3 volumes, facsimile, transcription, commentary (Moscow 1962)

Forbes, E. Ed. and rev., *Thayer's Life of Beethoven*, 2 vols. (New York 1963)

Hatten, Robert. *Musical Meaning in Beethoven: Markedness, Correlation, and Interpretation* (Bloomington 1994)

Jeffrey, B. Prefaces to *Beethoven: The 32 Piano Sonatas in Reprints of the First and Early Editions* (London 1989)

Johnson, Douglas, Alan Tyson and Robert Winter, *The Beethoven Sketchbooks* (Oxford 1985)

Kaiser, Joachim. *Beethovens 32 Klaviersonaten und ihre Interpretation* (Frankfurt am Main 1975)

Kamien, Roger. 'Aspects of the Recapitulation in Beethoven Piano Sonatas', *The Music Forum*, 4 (1976), pp. 195–236

Kerman, Joseph. 'Notes on Beethoven's Codas', in A. Tyson, ed., *Beethoven Studies*, 3 (1982), pp. 141–160

Kinsky, Georg., and Hans Halm, *Das Werk Beethovens: Thematisch-bibliographisches Verzeichnis seiner sämtlichen vollendeten Kompositionen* (Munich 1955)

Koch, H. C. *Musikalisches Lexicon* (Leipzig 1802)
Kurzgefaßtes Handwörterbuch der Musik für praktische Tonkünstler und für Dilettanten (Leipzig 1807; repr. Hildesheim 1981)

Komlós, Katalin. *Fortepianos and their Music: Germany, Austria and England, 1760–1800* (Oxford 1995)

Kramer, L. 'The Strange Case of Beethoven's *Coriolan*: Romantic Aesthetics, Modern Subjectivity, and the Cult of Shakespeare', *The Musical Quarterly*, 79 (1995), pp. 256–80

Krohn, I. 'Die Form des ersten Satzes der Mondscheinsonate', *Beethoven-Zentenarfeier* (Leipzig 1927), p. 58

Küthen, Hans-Werner. 'Beethovens "wirlich ganz neue Manier" – Eine Persiflage', *Beiträge zu Bethovens Kammermusik: Symposon Bonn 1984* (Munich 1987), pp. 216–24

Marx, A. B. *Anleitung zum Vortrag Beethovens Klavierwerke* (Berlin 1863; 2. 1875)

Mies, P. 'Quasi una Fantasia . . .', in S. Kross and H. Schmidt, eds., *Colloquium*

Amicorum: Joseph Schmidt-Görg zum 70. Geburtstag (Bonn 1967), pp. 239–49

Newman, William S. *The Sonata in the Classic Era* (Chapel Hill 1963)
'Beethoven's Pianos Versus His Piano Ideals', *Journal of the American Musiocological Society*, 23 (1970), pp. 484–504
Performance Practices in Beethoven's Piano Sonatas (New York 1971)
'Liszt's Interpreting of Beethoven's Piano Sonatas', *The Musical Quarterly*, 58 (1972), pp. 185–209

Prod'homme, J.-G. *Les Sonates pour Piano de Beethoven (1782–1823): Histoire et Critique* (Paris 1937)

Ratner, Leonard. *Classic Music: Expression, Form and Style* (London 1980)

Reinecke, Carl. *Die Beethovenschen Clavier-Sonaten* (Leipzig 1895)

Riemann, Hugo. *Ludwig van Beethovens sämtliche Klaviersonaten* (Berlin 1919)

Ringer, Alexander L. 'The Chasse as a Musical Topic of the Eighteenth Century', *Journal of the American Musicological Society*, 6 (1953), pp. 148–59
'Beethoven and the London Pianoforte School', *The Musical Quarterly*, 56 (1970), pp. 742–58

Rosen, Charles. *Sonata Forms* (London 1980)

Rosenblum, Sandra P. *Performance Practices in Classical Piano Music: their Principles and Applications* (Bloomington 1988)

Schleuning, Peter. *Die freie Fantasie. Ein Beitrag zur Erforschung der Klassischen Klaviermusik* (Göppingen 1973)

Schmalfeldt, Janet. 'Form as the Process of Becoming: The Beethoven-Hegelian Tradition and the "Tempest" Sonata', *The Beethoven Forum*, 4 (1995), pp. 37–72

Solomon, Maynard. *Beethoven* (New York 1977)

Tovey, Donald Francis. *A Companion to Beethoven's Pianoforte Sonatas* (London 1948)

Uhde, Jürgen. *Beethovens Klaviermusik*, 3 vols. (Stuttgart 1968–74)

Wallace, Robin. *Beethoven's Critics: Aesthetic Dilemmas and Resolutions during the Composer's Lifetime* (Cambridge 1986)

Index